KF

/494

Confessions of a New Age Dad

Confessions of
a New Age Dad

Paul Rhodes

EXPRESS NEWSPAPERS

This book first published in 2008 by
Express Newspapers
The Northern & Shell Building
10 Lower Thames Street
London EC3R 6EN

ISBN-13: 978-0-85079-362-8

Internal design and typesetting by Andrew Barker
Cover design, cover illustration, and internal illustrations by Richard Green
Edited by Laura Kesner

Printed and bound by SC International (Singapore)

For Edison

Acknowledgments

I would like to thank Geoff Marsh for championing me from the start; Fiona Tucker for her energy, enthusiasm, and faith in me; Laura Kesner for making me look good; Richard Green for the fantastic illustrations; my friends and family, especially my parents and my brother Kevin, for their belief in me; and my partner, Dianne, for her love and support.

Contents

Introduction

'Just what is a New Age Dad?' It's a question that my online editor, Geoff, asked me when I got the go-ahead to write this book. 'Because I know you, Paul, and you're not really New Age.'

I wasn't that taken aback by his rebuke because he's right. I'm not really New Age. I might be able to do the Sun Salutation and some other rudimentary yoga positions, but I don't sit at home crosslegged on a mat made of sustainable tree bark surrounded by crystals listening to a Songs of the Whale CD while trying to work out if my chakras are aligned. Yes, I often buy organic foods, my coffee is usually Fairtrade, and I do my best to recycle. I even have a compost bin at the end of my garden. However, I don't wear burlap sacks or shoes made from hemp and I've never been tattooed, branded or pierced. I didn't even bleach patches of my hair like many of my friends did in the 1980s (hey, Duran Duran did it – it was cool at the time).

No, in many ways I'm probably just an average bloke. I'm usually suited and booted when I go to work and I normally wear a T-shirt, jeans, and trainers when I'm not. I like a pint at the pub and I have been known to watch sport on television. I know how to change the spark plugs in a car, can do a little DIY (although I'd prefer not to – just ask my missus), and I know how to place an accumulator bet at the bookies. I can tell the same joke again and again and still find it funny (apparently something only men do, or so I've been told).

OK. So far, not so New Age. So how can I claim to be a New Age Dad? Well, I'll tell you.

It comes down to core beliefs. Ever since I received the news that I was going to be a dad I found the sense of responsibility that came with it overwhelming, but in a good way. I wanted to be a dad and I wanted to be the best dad I could be. I longed to be involved, every step of the way. I didn't want to be an impartial bystander who merely watched as Mummy ran herself ragged caring for the baby. No, I wanted to roll up my sleeves and muck in, even if that involved changing dirty nappies, wiping sick off the baby's chin, and getting up in the middle of the night to comfort a screaming infant. I needed to show this child that I cared. I had to show him that I loved him and always would. I didn't want to sit there passively while Mummy alone raised our child, so I made the conscious decision to make active fatherhood a major priority in my life. It's the many men out there who do the same who I consider to be New Age Dads.

To men of an older generation, raising children was primarily a woman's job. The man of the family was there to be the breadwinner and the authoritarian. There was a great distinction between the sexes and the roles they played and this was never more apparent than in parenting. The man made the rules and the woman made sure the children followed them.

In these more enlightened times – this 'New Age', if you will – I'd like to think mums and dads are equals and that's certainly the case in our household. Both Mummy and I have full-time jobs. The idea of childrearing and domestic chores being 'women's work' is not one either of us subscribe to and I'm sure this must be the case in most homes across the country.

So while the Supermum, the woman who enjoys a career and

still cares for her family, is celebrated, so too should the New Age Superdad. The man who works just as hard at his job as his wife or partner and then does his fair share of childrearing, too.

I know many new first-time fathers, like myself, who are just as busy with their domestic duties as they are at the workplace. Dads who get their children up in the morning and drop them off at school or nursery before heading to work. Dads who pick them up after a long day in the office and then feed them dinner, bath them, and put them to bed while mum is busy elsewhere. Dads who wake up and give the midnight feed so mum can get a good night's sleep. Dads who devote their entire weekend to their child so mum can have a break.

New Age Dads don't leave everything to their wives, girl-friends, and partners – they get involved. The extra responsibilities at home may make these men tired and worn out at times, and they may get frustrated and downcast too, but they wouldn't change a thing. They love being active dads and enjoy all the rewards that brings.

Being a New Age Dad isn't all about drudgery; fathers are now doing all the fun things that were once the preserve of mums – taking the children swimming, reading bedtime stories, and attending singing classes and baby massage lessons. A community centre local to me holds a post-natal parent and baby yoga session, which was originally set up for new mums. It soon became so full of dads that the men ended up getting their own class. New Age Dads aren't afraid to try things that they may have never considered before having children, and they're enjoying it.

While I believe there are a great many busy, fun-loving modern fathers like this out there, New Age Dad-hood is still something of an underground movement. Fatherhood and what comes with it is not talked about nearly as much as it should be. Men fear that they may be mocked or derided by friends or colleagues if they talk about their children. Worse still, some men think it's not manly to discuss it. What could be more masculine than being a hunter-gatherer, provider, carer, teacher, and protector of your children? It doesn't get more primal than that.

Being a New Age Dad is also, in some ways, arguably more difficult than being a mum. Motherhood is discussed openly and at length in the media and elsewhere but fatherhood is rarely mentioned. There is simply not the same amount of support available for dads as there is for mums. A new mother can ring her own mum when faced with a parenting dilemma but the same phone call from a New Age Dad to his father might be not be so useful.

It's time to acknowledge the greater role that fathers play today and, with this book, I hope to celebrate that. New Age Dads should be proud of their contributions and they should be applauded as loudly and as widely as mums.

I don't consider myself a vanguard of this fatherhood movement – there were many New Age Dads out there before I started writing this book and before I even became a dad myself – but I am a proud and happy member of this growing fraternity. I'm no childcare expert and although I have my own opinions and beliefs on parenting, I would never tell another family how to raise their children. It's simply not my place.

I'm just a bloke muddling along like many others, trying to do my best for my child and my family and enjoying successes and setbacks along the way. This book is simply my story. By telling it, perhaps it will help to open the dialogue between dads about the most fulfilling adventure life can offer – being a parent.

To all those New Age Dads out there making a difference, I salute you.

CHAPTER ONE

Preparing for D-Day

Picture perfect

There is that inevitable exasperated sigh people utter when a friend or colleague offers to show them a picture of their beloved child. You would think they were asking them to inspect a weeping, puss-ridden boil instead.

I suppose that I, too, used to recoil in horror when asked to look at such pictures. Before my partner became pregnant, that is. I'd say, 'Sure,' through gritted teeth and glance briefly at an image of their gurning child, covered in paint, mud, or food and missing the odd tooth. I would nod metronomically as the parent gave a brief précis of their child's history, including all vital statistics and major accomplishments from birth.

'He learned to tie his shoes last week,' the gleeful parent would proffer. Wow. I'm sure a spell as Director General of the United

Nations beckons, after he's cured cancer and climbed Everest backwards, twice, with his hands tied behind his back.

No longer do I take such a jaundiced view of children and parenthood. As an expectant father, I can't wait to be able to thrust snapshots of my child under the noses of family and friends and regale them with tales of the frequency and consistency of his stools and other fascinating tidbits I know they are desperate to hear. Even now, I've already started boring people to death with photos of my baby *in utero*.

My partner and I were both incredibly nervous ahead of her twelve-week scan – we were desperate for our child to be healthy. The womb is such a mystery that a paranoid mind like mine could invent as many nightmare scenarios as good ones. So we were relieved and elated when the ultrasound operator showed us a virtual picture of our little child and pointed out all the things that he was doing right: the head was big, so his brain was growing as it should; his heart was healthy and pumping away; he had two arms and two legs, and at some angles you could even see that he had a full complement of fingers, too. The operator then took a few still pictures for us to take home and in one of them it looks like the baby is actually waving at us, saying, 'Hello, I know you're watching! Don't worry, it's all good in here! See you in six months!'

Not only was I pleased to learn that the baby was developing normally, I was blown away by the fact that we could see him at all. Mummy's bump is still barely noticeable so it's difficult sometimes to imagine that there's a life growing inside her. But because of this scan and the grayscale images it has produced, we already know so much about our child and we have an actual picture of what he looks like. Instead of just being a foetus, some little tadpole-like creature swimming around in a lake of amniotic fluid within Mummy's tummy, by virtue of this picture he's already become a little person.

It has made me more able to come to terms with becoming a dad. The images have shown me the baby who will become part of my life in a few months' time. I have a picture of this person and, through having seen him wriggle and squirm, I can imagine what kind of personality he might have. I've read from his wave that he's pretty friendly and outgoing; he probably has a great sense of humour, too.

Now I can't stop staring at this image of my baby, and I love showing it off to everyone I know. I'm not even officially a dad yet and I have already developed one of the hallmarks of 'the annoying parent'. The scan pictures I have are more than just a tool with which to irritate family and friends. They have not only validated my child's existence as a human being, but they have also validated my role as his father.

Nesting instinct

I've never been one for doing things around the house. There's a coat rack that needs to be screwed into the wall by the front door. It has sat useless on the floor for about a year and a half, yet I still haven't got around to putting it up. This is partly because I think I'll mess it up and end up drilling holes in the wall that shouldn't be there and the coat rack will look skewwhiff and will eventually fall off and take huge chunks of the plaster with it.

I was therefore quite surprised at myself when I walked into the second bedroom of our small London house one day, three months before Golden Boy was due to be born, and decided that something had to be done. All of a sudden the room failed to fit my ideal of a nursery for my son. The bamboo-patterned wallpaper that covered one wall was vile, the lights equally distasteful, and the beige paint drab and dreary. How was my Golden Boy ever going to find comfort in a room this ugly? Impending fatherhood was bringing out the nesting instinct in me and, miraculously, it would turn me into something of a DIY god.

Knowing that Golden Boy would soon be released from the womb and joining us in the mortal world stoked a fire in me. I was certain that, once he was born, I would be incapable of accomplishing all of the improvements necessary to make our home perfect for life with a baby, what with the lack of sleep and demands of a child to cope with. I therefore vowed to fix up our abode myself and create a wonderful new environment for my son while I still had the chance.

Mummy, of course, was startled by this change and told me not to worry about taking on the work and that our home was already a satisfactory sanctuary for our child, but there was no stopping me. I was fired up with nesting fever and attacked the task of transforming the bedroom into a nursery fit for a prince with an energy never before seen.

Nothing was to be done by half measures, I told myself. When the hideous bamboo-print wallpaper refused to peel off in the easy manner I had expected, I hired a massive industrial stripping machine for the task, although the damage it caused meant I had to polyfilla huge chunks of wall afterwards. I put on not one but three coats of paint, a simple eggshell colour to help brighten the north-facing room. I then decided I might as well paint the adjoining bathroom and hallway. Since I was changing the wall-mounted light fixtures (there are now two child-friendly, lime-green ladybird-shaped lampshades above the cot), I thought I might as well remove those awful spotlights from the ceiling and install a new ceiling lamp, and then hook all of the lights up to a dimmer switch. Ambitious? Yes, but I had become DIY Dad, capable of anything!

Still, it wasn't enough. I was in a home improvement frenzy. I wanted to make life easier for Mummy and me as we began our parenting adventure, so I bought and installed a new dishwasher and a new washer/dryer. I put up some more shelves in the kitchen. I bought a new microwave and a new vacuum cleaner. I spent five hours putting together a new dresser from Ikea for Golden Boy's nursery. I invested in a new sofa, too, a leather one so that we could easily wipe off any mess the baby would make on it. My efforts could only be limited by the amount of room I had left on my credit card.

One long, arduous month and several thousand pounds later, I slumped on our new sofa, exhausted. Never before had I done so much work around the house (and never since, as Mummy will attest). I felt a huge sense of pride in my achievements. Not being the most mechanically minded of people (hey, I'm a wordsmith by trade – we generally don't like to get our hands dirty), I was highly impressed with myself.

I wasn't thinking rationally; it felt like I had been possessed. I was a crazed, testosterone-fuelled DIY freak hell-bent on preparing for the arrival of my first-born son. I suppose any anxiety I had about becoming a dad manifested itself in this nervous energy and empowered me to take on the world!

Golden Boy hadn't even been born and I was already experiencing all the primal urges and powerful emotions that fatherhood brings. It was then that I knew I was ready. I was the king of my castle. Bring on the arrival of the prince and heir.

The waiting is the hardest part

I had prepped the house, we had completed our antenatal course, our friends had thrown us a big, American-style baby shower, and my partner was fit to burst. I joked that she looked like a portly Bavarian with a love of beer, sausages, and schnitzel, so perfectly round was her belly. She didn't seem to find that funny. We had a birthing plan and a bag packed to take to hospital. Nine months had passed since conception night. We were as ready as could be for the birth of our first child; all we needed was for Golden Boy to make a move. So we waited ... and waited ... and waited ...

Mummy did an excellent job keeping herself in good shape and in good health while she was pregnant, so I suppose life in the womb was so pleasant for Golden Boy that he seemed reluctant to come out. He must have been reassured by the sound of the beating of his Mummy's heart and confident in the knowledge that, every few hours, copious amounts of cakes and ice-cream would be fed to him through the umbilical cord. (Our local bakery had never known such good business.)

He must have loved being swooshed around during Mummy's antenatal yoga classes and enjoyed hearing the muffled, disembodied voices of his parents speaking to him from outside the womb, singing and reading stories aloud. It must have been cosy, warm and comforting for him in there, because it seemed that, even after his forty-week term had been completed, he had no intention of ever leaving.

We were getting emails all the time from friends we had made at the antenatal parenting course to announce the births of their babies. Some had arrived a couple of weeks early, some had arrived a few days late, but none of their babies had wanted to spend as much time inside as Golden Boy. All the sitting around, waiting for the birth to happen, had my nerves in pieces.

The fact is that, unless you have a set date for a C-section, you have no idea when your child will arrive. If everything is seemingly normal, you have a rough one-month window in which you can safely assume he or she will emerge kicking and screaming into the world. So there's nothing else to do but sit back and wait. And, to quote Tom Petty, 'it's the waiting that's the hardest part'.

I was like a child counting the days until Christmas, full of nervousness and excitement, but not having any idea when Christmas would actually be. Although after nine months, I obviously felt pretty confident that it would be any minute. I'd phone Mummy constantly when I was at the office to ask her if she had felt any contractions. When I arrived home from work, I would put my head near Mummy's belly and ask Golden Boy if he had any plans to make his presence known. His silence said it all. Every night, as I lay in bed beside Mummy and waited for sleep, I would wonder if I would be woken in the middle of my slumber to be told, 'The baby's coming.' Night after night went by without a peep.

When we visited Mummy's GP, he assured us that everything was just fine. Golden Boy's heart was beating strongly and in no way was he distressed. He was just, to use a non-medical term, 'chillin''. If he was happy to stay in there, there was no need to disturb him. Well, not for a fortnight anyway.

Golden Boy was allowed the luxury of two further weeks in the womb before the doctors came to get him. Being induced to give birth was pretty far down on Mummy's list of fun ways to spend an evening – especially after some of the horror stories we had heard – so we hoped the threat of medical intervention would be the spur Golden Boy needed to 'engage' with the birthing canal and make his bid for freedom. But, as I now know, he doesn't like following orders.

The waiting continued. We tried to bring on the birth with all the normal methods (ie spicy food and sex, although not usually in that order) but still Golden Boy refused to budge. His willful belligerence was doing my head in as the inducement date crept closer and closer. Every day I was asked if we had given birth yet; anxious grandparents-to-be kept wondering what the hold-up was. Even Mummy was becoming fed up with having to lug around this great weight across her middle. None of this stress and anxiety bothered Golden Boy, who had barricaded himself inside Mummy. It appeared that if we wanted him, we would have to come and get him.

I'm normally a heavy sleeper and can remain unconscious through most disturbances, but on the night before we were due to head to the hospital to be induced, Mummy needed only six whispered words to get my full attention.

'Paul, I think I'm having contractions.'

The news came as much as a relief as anything else. Finally, I thought, let's get this show on the road.

Just like his dad, Golden Boy had waited until the last minute to get his act together.

CHAPTER TWO

The Arrival

Is this really how it's supposed to happen?

After sixteen hours of contractions, three warm baths, one unnecessary trip to hospital, and precious little sleep, it was time to return to the antenatal ward at our local infirmary, where we were told by a midwife that, despite all our efforts, Mummy still wasn't in labour. Could have fooled me.

Yes, Mummy was two weeks overdue and had been experiencing contractions since the early hours that morning but her water hadn't yet broken and, more importantly, she hadn't dilated more than a centimetre. So, in hospital parlance, she wasn't in labour. Apparently the midwives don't want to have to deal with you unless they can see the baby waving at them and threatening to pop out, which is why they had sent us packing when we pitched up at 3am earlier that day. Despite what we had thought were con- tractions happening at just five minutes apart, Mummy wasn't in labour. The midwives told us to come back that evening to be induced and, upon Mummy's insistence, we walked home. I had tried to persuade her to take a car to and from the hospital but she said she didn't want to be trapped in one if she was having a big, painful contraction and demanded that we make the ten-minute journey by foot. The look in her eye told me that it was not a good time to argue, so we braved gale-force winds and an encounter with an urban fox on a walk that I'll never forget. Mummy stopped every few hundred yards to lean against someone's house while she huffed and puffed through yet another contraction.

We returned to the antenatal ward that evening – again by foot – for the dreaded scheduled induction. It was a step we were keen to avoid but Golden Boy's reluctance to come out meant they were going in to get him, like it or not. The midwife on duty said she would give Mummy until 1am to keep trying before she would in- tervene. Then, as I was settling in for another long night of being the water-fetching, brow-mopping, bath-running, hand-holding, super-supportive birth partner that I was, the midwife said it was time for me to leave.

Now, attending the birth of a child is probably the most surreal event of most men's lives but, for me, it had just taken one hell of a bizarre twist. I wanted to be there to assist my partner through the whole birthing process. I wanted to see and experience every- thing along the way. I had waited nine and a half months for this to happen and was damned if I was going to leave right when we were on the final stretch. Everything I knew about childbirth I had learned, basically, from films and television. Nowhere had I seen dad being booted out halfway through the birth. So why on earth couldn't I stay? Is this how it really was supposed to happen?

'Dads are only allowed on the labour ward,' the midwife explained. 'This is the antenatal ward. Only when your wife is in labour will we move her upstairs, where dads are allowed, so you can't stay. But don't worry. We'll call you if anything happens. You won't miss the birth.'

Mummy was as stunned as I was but we didn't bother pressing the point any further – we had heard about what happens to parents who have ding-dongs with NHS midwives and didn't want to get on their bad side so early into the process. It might mean no help when we really needed it. I felt terrible for having to leave Mummy and for being totally excluded from part of what should be one of the best moments in my life but there was nothing we could do. The door, so to speak, had been closed. So I left poor Mummy on her lonesome on a cold hospital ward for what she later called the most painful and stressful night of her life and I wandered home in a daze.

I was left to wait and wonder what was happening in the hospital half a mile away. I could only pray that my partner and our baby were all right; I had no idea of knowing. Being left in the dark on such a momentous occasion is frightening. I had faith in the medical staff and that I would be told if anything significant happened, but that didn't make up for the fact that I wasn't there to witness it for myself or to help my partner. When I arrived home, I called the family to let them know what was going on and, having done that, I watched Match of the Day, drank a beer, and went to bed. That certainly wasn't part of our birth plan, but at that point, what else was a man to do?

I answered the phone on the second ring when it woke me at ten to six the next morning. Mummy said she had been moved upstairs, thus allowing me to be back by her side. I was so flustered I struggled to dress myself, but I was back on the ward twenty minutes later.

Never before had I seen my partner looking as tired and worn out as she did when I walked into her hospital room. She was mid-contraction, holding a gas-and-air dispenser in one hand and a midwife with the other.

'She's doing really well,' the midwife said, smiling at both of us once the contractions had finished. I thought Mummy was going to kill her.

'I've ordered a bloody epidural,' Mummy screeched, and it couldn't get there fast enough for both her and me. After it had been administered, Mummy seemed to relax and offered me a hit of her gas-and-air ('D'ya wanna try it? It's fun!'). The finish line was in sight.

However, nothing about this birth was straightforward. Golden Boy kept getting his shoulder stuck while trying to get through that bendy bit of the birth canal. He apparently needed a little help and if he became distressed, we were told an emergency C-section would be required. The doctors decided to 'prep' Mummy for a caesarean, just in case, and have the delivery 'in theatre'. What happened next was like a scene from ER. We went from having one midwife in the room with us to three, along with an anesthesiologist, an obstetrician, nurses, porters, and various people thrusting forms in front of Mummy to sign as even more analgesics were injected into her IV. I was told to scrub up and fol-low everyone into theatre, 'if I wanted to be there'. I wasn't missing this for the world.

Talk about excitement. The adrenaline was surging through me as I entered the operating theatre to be greeted by a sight I'm certain never to see again: Mummy lying there legs akimbo, with about a dozen men and women all having a good look. There is little time for dignity in the final stages of childbirth. I was amazed by all the people and equipment at the ready – all this attention on my beloved and the arrival of our Golden Boy.

'So this is why I pay taxes!' I thought. All that kit and all those people must have cost a lot of money, and I felt grateful and reassured knowing that each and every person and medical device was there.

Fortunately, the surgical gizmos were not required. I held Mummy's hand as a chorus of doctors, midwives, and nurses urged her to push and Golden Boy was born, with a little help from a ventouse device, minutes after we had arrived in theatre. It happened so fast that I ended up missing my opportunity to cut the umbilical cord, which was quite disappointing. I imagined it would be like a cabinet minister cutting the ribbon to open a new museum but one thousand times better: 'I declare this baby born.' Nevertheless, I got out the camera for the requisite seconds-old baby picture, Golden Boy's face all twisted as he howled at the brightness of the theatre's lights. (Mummy had previously informed me that there was no way I would be allowed to video anything to show to family and friends and that all photographic equipment had to stay at the north end at all times.) I quickly counted Golden Boy's fingers and toes before he was passed to Mummy for that all-important first cuddle. It was wonderful to behold but I couldn't wait to get my hands on him.

Finally, as the doctors and nurses turned their attentions back to Mummy, Golden Boy, swathed in white towels, was passed to me. I sat beside my partner and we admired this little life we had created in awe. Even at a healthy eight pounds plus, he was still so tiny, delicate, and fragile. It had been a long and strange journey to this point but none of that mattered. I was holding my healthy, first-born son. I had never felt more fortunate or proud. I stroked his teeny fingers and spoke to him softly as I tried to introduce him to his dad and to the world. I could barely think of what to say, so eventually I just stared at him instead, amazed by it all.

At last, he opened his eyes and looked at me for the first time.

What's wrong with the easy life?

One of the strangest messages of congratulations, if you could call it that, following Golden Boy's birth came from Mummy's antenatal yoga instructor. As was *de rigueur* for attendees of the class, Mummy sent out a round-robin email describing the birth and in the message admitted to having had an epidural and to needing the assistance of a ventouse device to deliver. While the other mums and mums-to-be emailed back their best wishes, the instructor, a Natural Birth Nazi, admonished my partner for not having a drug-free delivery, saying she would have managed the pain better if she had paid more attention to the breathing and relaxation techniques they had spent months practicing in class. As for the ventouse device, sacrilege!

Fortunately, Mummy didn't let that awful woman's comments bother her, unlike some of the other women who had attended her class and wanted desperately to have a perfect, natural birth. Mummy showed me an email that caused no end of upset for one classmate. In it, the Natural Birth Nazi condemned a new mum who ended up having an emergency C-section, saying she had given up trying for a natural birth too soon and that if she had persevered, she wouldn't have needed the surgery. She also said the mum should have put up a better fight against the recommendations of the doctors attending the birth. I was amazed. How could this Natural Birth Nazi cast aspersions on these mums?

The terrible rants from this crazed woman made me wonder what's wrong with the easy life? All of the dads I know weren't concerned whether their wives and partners had to take drugs or required a caesarean to give birth – their only worry was for the health and wellbeing of the mother and baby. So why is it that some women go out of their way to make others feel guilty or even like failures if they do not adhere to this strict, natural ethos?

Since when did giving birth become a competition, with those women failing to do it naturally, without pain relief, unworthy of calling themselves true women? If some women want to be natural birth martyrs, no matter what the cost, they can go for it. That is their choice. However, from all the many women I've spoken to and from the one birth I've attended, having a baby hurts like hell and some drugs to numb the pain can make the experience much more manageable. I remember seeing the change in Mummy after the pain relief from her epidural had kicked in; she looked like she had got her second wind. I know that the boost of energy she received when the pain eased helped her make it through the final push. If I was having a baby, I'd sure want one.

Me, I'm all for making things easier. However, I've found that some new mums seem to go out of their way to make life more difficult than it needs to be. This is certainly the case with those mums who insist on using cloth nappies. You won't find too many dads who want to faff around with these things.

At first, Mummy wanted us to use these bum-wrapping abominations, but as eco-friendly as I try to be, I wasn't having it. Who on earth wants to spend an evening washing out filthy nappies after having dealt with a baby all day? Not me. When Mummy explained to me that there are services that would deal with all the laundering issues for us, I still wasn't interested. I just wasn't convinced that cloth nappies could deal with the one major issue that stood out in my mind: leakage.

I know what cloth nappies look like and they don't have those protective gathers around the sides that the major disposable nappy brands like to advertise. Have you ever seen video footage where they pour a half-litre of fluid into a cloth nappy and it soaks up instantly but leaves the surface dry and never lets a drop of moisture seep through to the other side? No, neither have I. Case closed. Technology is designed to make life better so why not embrace it, I reasoned to Mummy. Surprinsingly, it's an argument I've actually won.

I may be a heretic to the eco cause but, to be frank, I'm not going to lose much sleep worrying about it. Every child born anywhere in the world will cause huge environmental damage, from the food they eat, the water they drink, the waste they make, and the carbon fumes they create through having the house kept warm and being driven and flown around. It doesn't seem to stop people from having kids. And nor should it.

Babies can be enough trouble as it. I'll take any shortcut to the easy life I can.

Just when will he do something?

There was all this excitement and anticipation leading up to the birth of my first child, these months filled with nervous energy, hopes, and dreams, all this time spent wondering what it will be like when the little one arrives. Then he was finally born and I felt this sense of jubilation and relief. I was overwhelmed with pride and counted my blessings. I felt so fortunate to have a healthy child, the only thing that really mattered. He was so amazing to me, purely for the fact that he existed.

That euphoria stayed with me for weeks as Mummy and I got

to know Golden Boy and became accustomed to managing a baby. It took some practice to get used to the basics, like changing his nappy. Once, my stepmum accused me of handling Golden Boy like a rabbit, the way I lifted up both his legs with one hand so I could slide his nappy underneath him with the other. Eventually, I learned what to do, our routine slotted into place, and Golden Boy began to fit seamlessly into our lives. Or rather, our lives began to fit around his. Babies don't really do consideration for other people, especially at four o'clock in the morning.

I'll admit that after a few months of watching this little man, I was beginning to get … well, bored at times. When I imagined life with a child I thought of all the fun things I could do with him: go swimming, have a kickabout in the park, feed the ducks, ride pushbikes, have long discussions about life and the universe and whatnot. Three-month-old babies, however, aren't really interested in any of that. All mine seems to want to do is lie there on a mat and, um, that's about it. Sitting around the house with a baby that's not really active isn't what I had in mind when I got into this fatherhood business. When is Golden Boy actually going to do something?

For the first three months, it didn't really matter much that Golden Boy wasn't Mr Excitement because we were so tired between feeds and nappy changes and requisite cuddles that we were happy just to watch him as he lay there, checking things out. However, I've started getting anxious for him to become more active. It's not like I expect him to learn the triple jump by next week but it would be great if he would at least crack a smile occasionally.

Milestones at this age seem miniscule. If we can put him on his gym mat (not as advanced as it sounds – it's a brightly coloured mat with two crossing arches above it from which soft toys hang) for five minutes without him suffering sensory overload and bursting into tears, then that's something to celebrate. Placing him on his tummy for a few minutes is another thing to cheer at. Any squawk or gurgle is received with a round of applause.

As far as entertainment goes, that's it. A fun day out for Golden Boy doesn't really seem to exist because on a trip to the supermarket in his pushchair I can guarantee that he'll be fast asleep before we even get there. Taking him to see the ducks at the park is just as pointless an expedition, as he almost always loses consciousness within minutes of leaving the house. Once, on a rare occasion when he did stay awake, we visited Hackney Farm to see the goats and chickens. Never before had I seen a child so disinterested in animals. I took him out of his pushchair at one point, held him in front of the turkey coop, and watched as a dozen birds rushed towards him, gobbling excitedly. What did Golden Boy do, I hear you ask? He turned his head to look at a tree, completely nonplussed by the feathered throng that gathered to greet him. It was the same with the pigs and the goats. What a waste of time.

I suppose I've failed to take into account just how much babies have to learn and how much the rest of us take for granted. We think nothing of being able to hold our heads upright, but at Golden Boy's age, when the head is the heaviest part of the body, trying to keep it steady is nigh on impossible. His neck muscles just haven't developed enough yet. Being able to articulate anything other than a cry requires the firing of many a synapse in his still growing and developing baby brain. Absorbing all of the information from the myriad activities going on around him – even dull things such as Mummy making a cup of tea or me unloading the dishwasher – is incredibly tiring.

Pretty much everything we do has had to be learned and that education takes a long time. I'm in my mid-thirties and my partner maintains that there are things I'll *never* learn. Perhaps I should give Golden Boy a break and accept that he'll get there in the end and in his own time. He certainly has a long way to go, but there is plenty of time for us to do all of the fun things I've imagined. I'm sure there will even come a time when I wish he'd be just like he is now – completely unquestioning and stays in the same place when I put him there.

The day I damaged the baby

It was a mistake, of course. Still, I felt more than just a pang of regret when the crimson blood dripped from his finger and stained the white of his Babygro.

My feelings of guilt and ineptitude were amplified when Golden Boy's little face screwed up, tears welled in his hazel eyes and a howl of pain, anguish, and disapproval emerged from his angry mouth. I passed him to Mummy for succor and he shot me a wearying look that seemed to say, 'Why, Daddy, Why?'

Mummy and I had been meaning to cut his fingernails for some time. Those tiny talons were capable of inflicting great wounds. His powerful, four-month-old fists relished clawing at my arms, tearing at my earlobes, and gouging at my eyeballs. Once, an exploratory digit found its way up my nose and its razor-like nail sliced open my nasal cavity as he withdrew it in a vicious manner. Let it be known that I was not the one to have drawn first blood.

The final straw came when we woke one morning to find a tiny graze across his left cheek, something he must have done while twisting in his sleep at night. The evidence of our neglect was plain for all to see. It would be embarrassing to take him that fateful morning to baby song and story at the library, knowing that all of the other parents would see that my son, however inadvertently, had self-harmed. I had to act.

However, trimming the fingernails of a baby is not the easiest of jobs. What appears to be a simple task is quite daunting when the area of concern is not much bigger than the head of a matchstick.

When I examined my son's hand it was difficult to see what to trim. I needed a magnifying glass to find those slivers of white, overgrown nail at the ends of his teeny fingers. It was a terrifying prospect – I was petrified of trimming them too far. I reminded myself that these millimetres of keratin could be considered weapons of mass destruction, to both him and to me. They had to be removed.

So I nominated Mummy for the role of talon trimmer. Mothers, on the whole, like taking charge of situations that concern their offspring and appear to have that innate confidence in dealing with the hurdles that emerge in the course of parenting. Basically, I didn't want the responsibility of operating the baby nail scissors, even if the blades were so dull they couldn't have scraped the burnt bits off toast.

Neither did Mummy, it seemed, as the days went by and his nails grew ever more fierce. I would give Golden Boy a cuddle and he would attempt to scythe great hunks of flesh from my neck or rip the lips from my face with his Edward Scissorhands-like grip. If Mummy wasn't going to do it, I had to take the bull by the horns and trim them myself.

I placed Golden Boy on my lap, wrapped my arm around him, and took his puny right paw in my hand. Starting with the little finger, I snipped ever so delicately and removed an almost invisible crescent of nail. I rubbed the end of the finger to check my handiwork and it was remarkably smooth. Dammit I was good at this!

Off came shards of nail on the ring and middle fingers, without a hint of struggle from Golden Boy, who sat calmly throughout the whole procedure. Then that almighty index finger presented itself to me, its nail of Freddy Krueger proportions. This sucker was so sharp you could carve your Sunday roast with it and, on several occasions, it had attempted to reap equal damage to my delicate visage. I was determined to cut it down to size. In my zealousness, I believe I may have taken off a smidge more nail than I meant to.

The wound only bled for about fifteen seconds, the crying stopped quickly, and a good ninety-five per cent of the nail was still attached to his finger, despite my crude trimming technique. The incident was soon forgotten by Golden Boy, we removed the bandage the following day, and my son still takes great pleasure in trying to poke my eye out with his index finger.

However, I will always be left with the guilty knowledge that it was me, his own father, who made him bleed for the very first time.

There's no such thing as a holiday with a baby ...

Mummy and I went online to book our holiday cottage in Wales for our first getaway with Golden Boy. We'd never had a break in the UK before. Usually, we'd book a flight to a foreign destination, either in Europe or further afield. We never bothered booking anywhere to stay and just used to see what we could find when we arrived. If we wanted to move on to somewhere new the following day, no problem – we could do as we pleased.

Now, however, we were beholden to the whims of Golden Boy. The thought of having to lug him and all of his clobber around somewhere new every day or two did not appeal. All that packing and unpacking – no thanks. So, seven days and nights in a homely cottage on the Pembrokeshire coast would have to do. A quiet rural idyll would, I imagined, be the perfect way to relax and unwind after the chaos created by the arrival of a newborn. However, when I was booking the break, I didn't realise that unless you have a nanny or a doting grandparent in tow, there really is no such thing as a holiday with a baby.

Of course we were not planning to spend all of our time holed up in a small, moderately appointed abode. We planned to take day trips and enjoy as much of the beautiful outdoors as Wales has to offer. But it was June and we were in Britain so it wasn't a huge surprise when the heavens opened just as we crossed the Severn Bridge. The fact that it stayed this way for the entire week perhaps won't come as a shock either. Nor should the fact that, by the time we had crossed the border into Wales, Golden Boy had had more than enough car travel for one day. With another 100-odd miles to go, it was through gritted teeth and perforated eardrums that we made it to our final destination.

The holiday let had everything it promised on the website and more – the view of the sea was definitely there. From the veranda we could see the Pembroke Estuary and the Cleddau Bridge beyond, as well as Pembroke docks and the Texaco oil refinery. Eat your heart out, Côte D'Azur! And in the well-laid-out suite was enough media to keep us entertained for the week. The John Thaw video collection and novels by Jeffery Archer, Judith Krantz, Jilly Cooper, and Jackie Collins could have made a bonfire that would be seen in Cardiff and with the weather the way it was, a roaring fire didn't seem like such a bad idea.

Mummy and I would have been quite happy to brave the ele-

ments on a quaint coastal path for a few hours, but hiking along
slippery trails in the rain with a sodden Golden Boy in tow was
not so appealing. And since I had (perhaps foolishly) put a ban on
television – I thought it might force Mummy and I to do something more productive and spend more 'quality time' together
– we were hard pressed for things to do. Without the prospect of
a Morse marathon, and sensing our boredom on day two of our
break, Golden Boy decided to liven things up – with a three-hour
screaming fit.

This episode was surprising in that Golden Boy almost never
cries. Sure, he's yelled and moaned and complained to get his
point across, but in the four and a half months since his birth,
he's never cried for hours on end without reason. After careful
inspection, we could not understand what the problem was. This
had Mummy and me worried. We didn't know what to do. Trying
to feed and comfort him didn't work and after hours of panicked
parenting, we thought the worst and took him to hospital. This
might appear to be an extreme reaction but new parents do weird
things. Golden Boy didn't let up once during the half-hour drive
to the Withybush Hospital in Haverfordwest, so it seemed we had
made the correct decision.

Entering pretty much anywhere with a screaming baby is
bound to get you attention and the casualty ward of a hospital is
no different. We were instantly at the front of the queue and had
doctors inspecting him to find the source of his mystery ailment
within minutes of our arrival. They were also quick to convince
us that we were right to bring him in, even though they struggled
to find anything wrong with him. It didn't appear to be wind, he
wasn't constipated, and he hadn't, thank goodness, experienced
any colic before. He didn't have a temperature, a cough, or any
congestion. He hadn't been sick or passed out. He wasn't hungry or dehydrated. The doctors couldn't find any symptoms that

would precipitate his prolonged outburst, so they were as baffled as we were. Still, Golden Boy wailed like he had been shot, so he was moved upstairs to the children's ward. It was there that a medic noticed something unusual.

'How long has he had these marks?' she asked us, holding up Golden Boy's leg for inspection. Neither Mummy nor I had noticed them before and we instantly felt like parental failures for not picking up on them. Had they been there when we changed him that morning? We couldn't remember.

'It could be meningitis' the doctor said.

I needed to check my hearing to make sure I had heard him correctly. Meningitis? I didn't really know what it was, never mind how Golden Boy could have contracted it. All I knew was that it sounded bad and that I didn't want to get it and I wouldn't want my son to have it either. Panic set in.

'Don't worry, it might not be,' the doctor added, 'but we'll want to watch him for a while and do some tests.'

It sounded reasonable. We waited anxiously while the doctors and nurses milled around and filled in charts before leaving us alone. Then Golden Boy did the most incredible thing: he stopped crying. He had been at it for almost four and a half hours, but it seemed, upon discovering his prognosis, he decided to perk up. With the disappearance of tears and howls went that mystery rash, too, vanishing from his body in a matter of minutes. When the head nurse returned she seemed to think Golden Boy was OK as well, and wasn't suffering from meningitis. It could have been an allergic reaction to something in the cottage. Who knew? These odd occurrences are common in babies, she told us, adding that, since he didn't have a fever or any other dangerous symptoms, we could probably all go in a hour or two and resume our relaxing holiday. Things are never that simple, though. Golden Boy was back to his normal, entertaining self, making all the nurses and doctors smile with his effortless baby charm, but that wasn't enough to win him a reprieve from the intrusive methods of the senior medical staff. Golden Boy wasn't going anywhere, the head of paediatrics said. It still might be meningitis, even if that was a pretty big 'might'. Not only would my son need to give a blood sample, he would have to stay overnight. Our holiday was getting better by the minute.

Taking a blood sample from a baby is, I was told, very difficult and holding my son's tiny hand in place while a trainee doctor jabbed a needle into the top of his fist and rooted around for a vein that was about one-tenth of the diameter of a string of spaghetti had to be one of the most difficult things I've witnessed as a new parent. (Mummy, who has a phobia of needles, flat out refused to attend this horrific event.) To explain how excruciatingly awful it was, the nurse made the trainee stop after she had failed to squeeze an adequate sample from my son's hand despite trying for what seemed like twenty minutes. My son was being treated like a cross between a guinea pig and a pincushion and I was beginning to suspect that they were keeping him there merely to serve as a real-life practice doll. However, at this point, who was I to argue? Finally, a more senior doctor came in and showed the trainee how it was done on Golden Boy's other, previously untouched hand, leaving one paw battered and bruised and a tube hanging out of the other in case an IV had to be hooked up later. To keep him from scratching it or pulling the tube out, his entire lower right arm was wrapped in a massive bandage. Mummy thought he had a cast on when we returned from the treatment room.

The blood-taking ordeal, coupled with the excitement of the day, wore the three of us out. So while Golden Boy crashed out in his capacious hospital cot, Mummy and I curled up on a mattress on the floor in a corner of his room. It's funny how holiday moments like this are never mentioned in the brochures. The rain seemed more like a minor quibble by now.

Fortunately, the test results came back negative and the doctors deemed Golden Boy fit to leave the ward the next morning. Our medical scare was over. My son hasn't cried like that since, so I imagine he's learned his lesson. The doctors insisted we continue our fun-filled holiday and released us into the grey, dreary world. It was still raining, so we returned to the confines of our cottage. I looked out at the glow of the pilot flame burning atop some kind of tower high above the oil refinery, an orange beacon against the dark sky. With my TV fatwa firmly in place, Mummy and I ended up taking Golden Boy on long drives in the car and we completed an intricate 1,000-piece puzzle that took the best part of three days. It was the highlight of the trip. That and the great holiday snap of Golden Boy thrashing about in his hospital cot with a huge tube sticking out of his arm.

The rain did eventually stop for about four hours on the day before we left, and we managed a walk and a couple of beers on the deck, where we soaked up the rays and those stunning industrial views. I almost managed a tan. The next morning it was time to set off on the long drive home.

I think it was the first holiday I've ever had where I was glad for it to end. Wales is a beautiful country and has wonderfully kind attentive people working in its hospitals. But after our ordeal, I'm not sure we'll be heading back again any time soon. I just hope it's not a prototype for holidays to come.

Pint-sized fun
at the pub

To be fair to Golden Boy, I suppose it wasn't all gloom and doom on our Welsh adventure and I did manage to take better photographs than the ones I have of him in the infirmary. The funniest snapshot I took was of him in a pub in St David's. Looking like a wild-eyed mini-hooligan in his hoodie, Golden Boy is desperately trying to grab a half pint of beer and a packet of peanuts on the table in front of him. Mummy blames that thirst for ale on my side of the family.

While we were on holiday in this wet but wonderful part of the world, we visited a number of excellent, family-friendly pubs. I had never really noticed these places before. I mean, even three or four years ago, how often would you see a baby in a pub? Almost never. The landlords of these establishments we visited, however, had no problem with Mummy and me bringing along our infant son while we enjoyed lunch or a cheeky pint in the afternoon. One publican didn't even bat an eye when Mummy went to a quiet corner in the back of his hostelry to breastfeed Golden Boy and change his nappy. I mention this because I was quite surprised by how welcoming and progressive these pubs were. I never expected to take my son down the boozer at such an age.

Pubs seemed so taboo to me when I was a child. They were places for adults only. I remember visiting my grandparents in Norfolk in the 1980s, and there was one pub close to them, The Black Swan, that had a play space for children out the back – but there was no way children were allowed inside. It seemed exciting to me just being able to get that close to this mythical place where adults got up to goodness knows what, even if I never managed to venture through the big oak-and-glass doors.

In the wake of the smoking ban and these more enlightened attitudes, the pub seems not such a bad place to go with a child. Nowadays, many hostelries that serve food look like crèches on the weekend, with babies screaming and children running all over the place. Many pubs we've been to even have highchairs available. With the smokers forced outside, I suppose publicans are trying to appeal to a new, lucrative market: stressed-out parents in need of a glass or two to chill out.

Mummy and I haven't made a habit of taking Golden Boy to the pub – somehow, still, it just doesn't seem right – but it is nice to know there are a number of places where we can enjoy a pie and a pint with our son in tow without impunity.

Getting to Know You

Golden Boy makes an impression

I am a member of the Tate and have been for the past five years or so. I woke up one day and thought that, since I lived in London, I should get more out of being in the capital. I should indulge myself in 'cultcha'. So I signed up for membership at the Tate and, for the privilege, I get free tickets to shows I never go to and a quarterly magazine that I never read.

And every March I get a letter telling me that, unless I instruct them otherwise, they are going to plunder my bank account for another £68 because they have my details at hand. Since I like the members lounge at Tate Modern – which is on the sixth floor and has great views across the Thames to St Paul's, the City, and beyond – I never bother cancelling the direct debit. So, basically, I spend £68 a year to be able to sit in a nice spot, drink cappuccinos, and impress friends and family who don't live in London.

Then, one day last week, I woke up and thought that, since I live in London, I should get out more and enjoy some culture. Just because I am now a dad with a small child doesn't mean I have to be a shut-in whose highlight is to see how many fabulous day-time television shows I can watch in one go. No, instead I would take my family out to look at art. Golden Boy had never in his six months been to an art gallery. It would be another first to register. I was sure he'd be thrilled.

I picked up the Tate magazine I normally don't read and looked to see what was on. There was a photography exhibition that caught my eye at Tate Britain, the old building in Pimlico that barely anyone goes to anymore now they've built the big new one on the South Bank. Photography seemed more exciting to me than the different coloured fluorescent lights, tinned elephant dung, and all that other ridiculous modern art malarkey they tend to line the walls with, so I decided that we should give it a go.

The problem I have with art galleries is that no one – myself included – knows what the true etiquette is when you wander around them. If they don't rope off an area, just how close are you allowed to stand to a work? And for how long? And just how much noise are you allowed to make? Some people think that an art gallery is akin to a library, where silence is king, while others have no qualms bellowing to their mate at the other end of a great hall to inquire whether they have revelled in the spiritual magnificence of a Delacroix or whatever. I try to keep a happy medium and on this trip my mission was to attempt to stifle any extraordinary outbursts from Golden Boy, whose knowledge, understanding, and appreciation of fine photography is, at this early stage in his life, limited.

He was good and indulged his parents for forty-five minutes or so before deciding he had seen enough art for one day. Out of courtesy for the art-lovers around us, we were obliged to leave and so we retired to the cafeteria for the requisite cappuccino and slice of cake. They do a nice coffee and slice of cake at the Tate. The views at the Tate Britain cafeteria are non-existent – it's underground – but Mummy and I felt good to have got out of the house. And if we were really lucky, we still might get home in time for Countdown.

With a baby in tow, it is madness to leave anywhere without a nappy change first and since I had so kindly suggested this outing, and paid for coffee and cake, it was Mummy's job to manage it. So I sat in my comfortable chair and pondered the photography I had just seen while Mummy and Golden Boy headed to the baby change facilities. I had been so soothed by my bout of culture that I actually fell asleep and was only woken by an irritable kick from Mummy upon her return. Since I was a bit out of it, it took a minute or so before I noticed Mummy was wearing a different shirt.

Apparently, while heading to the loos, there had been an accident. Mummy was carrying Golden Boy, with his cute face poking over her shoulder. A loud squirty noise then emitted from our son's bottom. When the two older ladies who had followed Mummy into the toilets exclaimed, 'What a lovely baby!' she was able to turn around and reveal to them the liquid poo artwork Golden Boy had created – all down her once white top.

One trip to an art gallery and already my son was an abstract impressionist. When people say babies pick up on things quickly, I now know what they mean.

He ain't heavy ...

I think Mummy bought the baby backpack because she was hoping it would help me finally shift the weight I put on during my sympathetic pregnancy. It would be good exercise, she declared, for me to have Golden Boy strapped to my back when we went out for walks.

You see, these days it is no good to go for a stroll with the baby riding comfortably in a pushchair. No, to prove you are a loving yet macho dad, you have to carry the child in a device attached to your body. You can then show that you are not afraid to have close physical contact with your offspring and that you have the strength to lug him around for hours on end.

In the first few months after birth this isn't a problem; babies don't weigh very much. However, once they outgrow the popular Baby Bjorn device that holds the child to your chest, transporting him or her under your own steam isn't nearly as fun.

As a trip to London's Borough Market or any other place where you can get organic mangoes and £20 bottles of balsamic vinegar will show, the vast number of baby backpacks bouncing about proves that there are plenty of dads trying to show how tough yet caring they really are. And how flush they are, too. Some of these baby backpacks go for more than £150. Fortunately, Mummy is resourceful and managed to find one on eBay for £5.53 (it cost us more to have it shipped).

For that price we don't have one of these fancy new lightweight carriers made of Kevlar or other space-age metals in a tasteful neutral tone, but a hulking great blue thing with a massive aluminium frame that looks like it spent the last thirty years in the lost and found box at a Katmandu hostel.

So now my son can ride along behind me and practice his conga drum technique on the top of my head while I search for pecori-

no cheese and rare breeds of parsley. He loves it, Mummy says, though I'll have to take her word for it, as I can't see him. Isn't the fact he's enjoying himself the only thing that matters anyway?

Meanwhile, it makes an afternoon's meandering feel more like a military training exercise, with twenty-odd pounds of baby boy kicking and wriggling on my back and shrieking with equal parts terror and delight in my ear. Central London is about as baby friendly as a chemical weapons factory, so transporting a child in a baby backpack isn't without its hazards.

Like Kate Moss, I enjoy browsing the stalls of Spitalfields Market on a Sunday, a task which used to be quite enjoyable with a pushchair. Wherever I went, the crowds would part like the Red Sea did for Moses. It was no problem to navigate through the hordes of shoppers in search of handknitted jumpers made from Andean llama wool. People always made room for us. Plus I could put my keys, mobile phone, jacket, and the Fairtrade coffee beans I had bought in the basket underneath the seat.

As soon as I put Golden Boy on my back, I became another annoying person with a huge bloody backpack clogging up the marketplace. People felt no guilt in pushing, shoving or elbowing me out of the way if I stood between them and some Queen olives stuffed with pimento, never mind that there was a little person clinging to my shoulders (and my ears). One woman with the gait and manners of a carthorse barged right into me, nearly knocking me over. Of course, only a weak 'sorry' was offered as means of apology before she trotted off again.

No, the hassle of the baby backpack is not for me. If Mummy thinks I need to shed a few pounds, we'll have to consider lipo-suction instead. From now on, when I'm making my way through the urban jungle, I'll take out the ankles of anyone who gets in the way of my pushchair and me.

Getting to Know You

Old habits die hard

My son is becoming a prolific thumb-sucker. Like many of his habits, it seemed so innocuous at first.

He would do it to comfort himself just before he fell asleep. He looked so cute I thought nothing of it. However, his habit started escalating. He would suck his thumb when he was experiencing teething pains (nearly three months on and still no teeth). He did some supplemental thumb sucking when he was hungry. Like an addicted smoker, he'd do it again when he was bored, nervous or mildly agitated and wanted a moment to chill out and reflect.

Now he is a full-blown thumb addict, stuffing it into his gob at any idle moment. What once seemed adorable now has me worried. I have frightening visions of him being like Linus in the Charlie Brown cartoons, the maudlin, comfort-blanket-snuggling, thumb-sucking introvert who laments life's inequalities. I'm worried my son is turning into a wimp.

I want Golden Boy to grow up to be strong, confident, bold, and daring, like the Formula One driver Lewis Hamilton. How is my son going to become a leader of men when his mouth is full of thumb?

I started investigating the prospect of giving him a dummy. My stepmum had suggested we try it; both her boys had dummies as children and were the better for it, she said. A GP friend of mine had sent a picture of his boy munching on a dummy, so leading medical advice must deem it OK, too. Another friend of ours says their little bundle of sunshine can't manage the agonies of teething without one. Who am I to refuse my son a dummy?

Like everything else in the realm of parenting, however, there is so much conflicting advice.

The lovely ladies who run the Friday baby massage class (I

thought Golden Boy could learn some tips to loosen up the tension in my shoulders but it turns out that I'm the one who has to do all the work) said I shouldn't give him a dummy, as it may well stunt his verbal development. I wouldn't want to stop him from babbling away like he does now, especially while he's stuck on 'Dada', would I? I see what they are saying, but how can anyone talk with a big fat thumb in their mouth?

There is also the worry that a dummy might ruin his teeth, although that, too, is a concern with thumb sucking. However, a dummy will be long gone before his permanent gnashers come in, and that will hopefully prevent me from having to stump up for a hefty orthodontic bill when he reaches his teens.

I was convinced that a dummy was the way forward. However, I met an impervious obstacle that stopped theory from becoming reality. Mummy said 'no', suggesting that dummies are filthy, germ-ridden devices that are as addictive as thumbs. 'It's something we'll struggle to take away from him later,' she warned. Surely we'll just chop off his thumbs if he objects to our pleas to stop slurping on them when he gets older. Two colleagues admitted to me last week that they sucked their thumbs until they were fifteen! We could not let that fate befall our son. Still, my argument didn't hold much sway with Mummy. Since I don't like sleeping on the sofa, I haven't pursued it. The thumb sucking continues apace.

On Monday we were in Ikea, a destination I would not recommend to anyone mid-term-time. In the cafeteria I saw a boy of around four queuing with his mummy for some Swedish meatballs. He was sucking furiously on his thumb and clutching a teddy bear to his chest.

Now, I'm sure he is a wonderful, sensitive child, and could go on in life to write some beautiful poetry or set up a charity or become a social worker or teach children maths and English in some deprived village in Africa. But I know that, during the intervening years to adulthood, he will be picked last for football every time or worse and that will be hard for him.

Even though my son is a mere seven and a half months old and thumb-sucking is said to be perfectly normal at that age, I watch anxiously every time he raises the digit to his mouth. I've come to realise so much of parenting is trying to prevent what we fear for ourselves from happening to our children.

Toying with an education

There is a section of our lounge where we had planned to put a big, comfy chair and a reading lamp. It would be an oasis of relaxation, where one could get stuck into a meaty novel and a fine malt of a winter's evening. Then Golden Boy arrived and the area has been over-run by toys ever since. Our dream of a literary corner has all but died.

For someone who's been on the planet for less time than he spent in the womb, Golden Boy sure has a lot of possessions. He has enough stuffed animals to fill an ark, loads of rattles and mirrors, squidgy toys, crinkly toys, plush toys, and bendy toys. Fortunately, friends and indulgent grandparents have fronted most of the cost of this extravagance.

Still, it is Mummy and me who have to find the space to put it and this is most annoying, especially when he barely plays with any of it. We've all been duped by the educational toy scam.

These days, a toy is not simply a toy; it is an implement of learning that will, we are told, have a lifelong bearing on our child's growth and development. In the competitive world of modern parenting, you can't afford to have your child left behind.

Twenty years ago it would have been good if your son could count to ten, recite the alphabet, and know the names of all the different colours by age four. Kids nowadays need to have five languages under their belts, be masters of international diplomacy, and play piano concertos by Brahms with panache.

Being void of these skills could label your child 'educationally sub-normal', as an acquaintance's seemingly normal three-year-old daughter was deemed to be last week when she was assessed for a nursery place. Her parents are both top corporate lawyers. If education professionals think these high-fliers' kid is a thicko, what chance do the rest of us have?

Therefore, we've invested in Golden Boy's mind by providing him with an array of educational toys to engage his senses. One such toy, a clutch cube (basically a brightly coloured soft square with a bell in the middle and a couple of rings hanging off the side) is designed to 'stimulate curiosity', 'encourage interaction', and 'awaken imagination'. Thank goodness.

My son will marvel at this innovation for all of two minutes, but if I give him an envelope with a window in the front or an old catalogue to destroy, I've got him amused for half an hour, at least. The cube, one of the smaller and less expensive items we've purchased, cost close to fifteen pounds; the envelopes and catalogues come free through the post nearly every day. Maybe I'm educationally sub-normal for splashing out fifteen quid on a toy that barely maintains my son's interest when there is free stuff around us that I know does the job of stimulating curiosity, encouraging interaction, and awakening his imagination just fine.

An array of 'toys' that Golden Boy finds infinitely fascinating include: a plastic bowl and spoon; the TV remote control (taking the battery out first is a must, or viewing the show you want at the correct volume becomes a problem); a pillow; a T-shirt; and an old mobile phone. Those and a stack of new library books every couple of weeks and you could virtually cut the so-called educational toy load by about two-thirds and still keep baby entertained and, most importantly, developing brain cells. All this at about a third of the cost.

Once, a couple of months ago, Golden Boy started deliberately hitting himself in the head with the TV remote control. He did it harder and harder until it hurt him enough to make him cry. He's never done it since and prefers instead to just press all the squidgy buttons and to wave it in the air. Clearly that was a sharp learning curve for him and a lesson learned that will stand him in good stead for life.

The daddy of all hangovers

Our selfish modern fixation with youth means that many people of my generation try to avoid growing up. Believe me, I put it off for as long as possible. A concert promoter I met last spring told me, 'These days, twenty-nine is the new nineteen. People just want to go out and have fun'. I believe he's right. Escapism is an easy option for people frightened, like I was, by the thought of settling down. Anyway, it made me feel good to think that, according to his logic, I was still in my twenties.

The thing is, adult life has a way of catching up with you, whether you like it or not. Well, it did for me. Now I'm a family man I have to change dirty nappies on a regular basis. I have de-

pendants, a mortgage, a pension, credit card repayments, more
than a few grey hairs, something that can be loosely described as
a career ... and, it appears, many leaves to rake up in the garden.
All things I never dreamt of five or ten years ago. The carefree
pleasures of my youth sometimes seem a million miles away.

This isn't to say that my new, responsible adult life is drudgery.
Far from it. There are many wonderful things to experience, like
the joy of watching my son rocking back and forth on his hands
and knees, knowing that any day now he'll be crawling across the
living room floor.

As any parent who juggles work and family life knows, things
are much more hectic than when you were free and single. You
have to plot and plan. You have to stay organised. There is little
room for spontaneity, the favourite word of people who only have
to think of themselves. At times, this can make me more than a
little winsome for those heady days when all I had to worry about
was wearing the right pair of trainers and being cool.

Maybe that was the reason I decided to take Mummy to see
the Foo Fighters at London's O2 Arena on Sunday night. It would
provide us with an opportunity to break free from our routine
and let our hair down a bit. More importantly, it would give us a
chance to feel young again. So, rebel to the core, I donned a pair
of jeans, a black T-shirt and some damn cool trainers and trudged
out to North Greenwich in the rain and the cold to do something
I used to do with alarming regularity – pay a lot of money to stand
in a large room with loads of sweaty, smelly people and become
slowly deafened.

Clawing ourselves away from our workaday life took some doing. Walking into an arena filled with people half my age did make
me feel a bit old. It wasn't until we received notice, by text, to say
that Golden Boy was all tucked up and sleeping soundly that we
really started to relax. I then had to tell Mummy off for reading a

report that had been emailed to her Blackberry. You know you're old when your 'crackberry' holds more interest for you on a night out than anything else.

However, by the time the opening acts finished their sets and the Foos made their way to the stage, an almost magical transformation was happening: we were reverting to our former carefree selves. Aided by a couple of over-priced lagers, we were dancing and singing along as the Foos ploughed through their catalogue of hits. We even had spied people older than us doing the same, which was in itself reassuring.

Reality came rushing back at 6am the following morning, when Golden Boy decided to make his presence known. Despite my hoarse throat, chronic tiredness, and the ringing in my ears, it's good to know I can still party with the best of them. I may not be a young man anymore but I'm happy to pretend. I'm fairly certain that Golden Boy will find me excruciatingly embarrassing when he gets older, but isn't that the point of being a dad?

Making a meal out of feeding baby

It was a delicious dinner, if I do say so myself, and one that had taken me some time to prepare. It was worth it alone for the wonderful smell that filled the house.

When I took the hotpot out of the oven, the tender hunks of lamb flecked with fresh rosemary looked gloriously succulent in their warm bed of vegetables and potatoes. I was ravenous and thought I'd sneak a bite, when Mummy walked into the kitchen and caught me.

'Leave that alone,' she scolded, 'that's for the baby.'

As penance for my greed, Mummy made me purée the lot, turning a lovely adult-ready meal into a squishy, baby-friendly pulp.

For someone not even nine months old, Golden Boy has already developed a taste for the finer things in life. He's a true gourmet. This week, as well as the lamb hotpot, he's been treated to chicken risotto, leek and courgette soup, and mini fish pies, all homemade and with organic ingredients that yours truly spent ages sourcing.

'It must be organic,' Mummy implores, before shipping me off to the supermarket in search of pesticide-free fruit and veg. 'Only the best for our child.'

Yeah, and only the most expensive, too. (Mummy refuses to let me buy jars of baby mush because, 'they're filled with crap'.)

In the first six months of his life, Golden Boy was breast-fed almost exclusively, which is the best option for babies and daddies alike. If my son woke up in the middle of the night, all I had to do was push Mummy out of bed to deal with the situation because I knew I lacked the necessary equipment to pacify our child.

Once we started weaning him, life changed rather dramatically. Sure, Golden Boy began to sleep through the night but the baby management workload almost trebled for Mummy and unfortunately I was roped in to help out.

As much as he loves his food, Golden Boy still spends hours and hours eating each lovingly prepared meal. It's amazing how he can watch me scoop the food out of the bowl, but his attention gets diverted when the spoon is mere inches from his mouth. I can see him thinking, 'Wow, Daddy's wearing trousers today,' 'Hey, there's that tree out in the garden again,' and 'Ooh, I've got a foot!'

Despite our attempts, he refuses to feed himself. 'Why bother,' he thinks, 'when there are two people here to feed me? I'll just mash that broccoli between my fingers and then throw it on the floor.'

I worked out that at three meals a day, Golden Boy spends twenty-one hours a week eating. Then tack on time for preparing each meal, buying the extra organic nosh, and doing the additional laundry that comes with feeding a baby (thank God he's stopped that 'I'm-going-to-smoosh-every-other-mouthful-into-my-sleeve' trick he was so fond of). That means we spend at least one twenty-four-hour day every week simply feeding him.

While all this top-quality tucker has helped make Golden Boy the happy, healthy, rosy-cheeked baby he is, it has reduced Mummy and me to a knackered set of galley slaves, skivvying after a miniature Henry VIII with an ever-expanding appetite. If he's the slightest bit hungry, boy does he let you know about it.

After standing over a hot stove all day, steaming and purée-ing a never-ending array of vegetables for Golden Boy (butternut squash is his favourite, since you ask), we really can't be bothered to cook for ourselves. He may get the best money can buy but it's takeaways and beans on toast for us, slumped in front of repeats of Desperate Housewives. Trust me, I know how desperate they feel.

Goaded on by lashings of middle-class childrearing guilt served up by baby nutrition experts like Gina Ford and Annabel Karmel, our organic, home-cooked odyssey continues apace. It means yet more effort on our part that Golden Boy will probably never really appreciate or thank us for. Then again, gratitude isn't something I've come to expect as a parent.

Childrearing is a competitive business

Golden Boy enjoys an active social life. This is as much to get me out of the house in the morning as it is to allow him to interact with other babies. It also gives me a chance to check out the competition.

Parents of young children are desperate for them to reach their milestones as soon as possible and preferably before other members of their peer group. This is the reason parents gather at various play groups – so they can show off their little ones' latest achievements.

I first noticed this at baby massage, when Golden Boy was three months old and had just learned to turn himself on to his front.

'He's rolling over already, is he?' one of the mums asked, before turning to look despairingly at her poor, motionless child of the same age. 'He doesn't like to be on his tummy.'

I could tell that she was already worried, at such an early stage, that hers would be a baby that would never crawl. She was frightened that all those mental images she had of her child scampering across the living room rug on his hands and knees would never materialise in real life. It was sad, to say the least.

In my experience, it is women who tend to be the most competitive, as they try to out-mum each other at every opportunity. This is most apparent when it comes to weaning. As soon as these children hit the magical six-month mark, the age at which experts say it is best to introduce real food, it becomes a race to see who can get their baby off the boob and on to solids first – I suspect the mums want to get back on the wine and G&Ts without the fear or guilt of harming their babies through boozy breast milk.

'I've dropped another breast feed,' one mum proudly announced at our baby massage class one morning as she championed her chunky son as a paragon of eating.

'Really,' the other mums scowled.

'Well, *my* daughter just loves finger food and is feeding herself,' said another mum, in a display of one-up-mum-ship.

There was the potential for things to turn nasty quickly, so I decided to stay out of it.

With dads, however, there doesn't seem to be the same level of intense rivalry as with the mums, though I'm sure that will all change in a few years time, when we're standing on the sidelines of a sport field, watching our kids chasing a ball around. Recently, another dad asked me if Golden Boy had started crawling, like so many of the slightly older children who regularly attend our story time group.

'No, not yet,' I told him. 'Almost.'

His eyes radiated silent empathy as he watched his daughter kick and wiggle on the floor.

'How old?' he asked.

'Just over eight months.'

'She's nine-and-a-half months and nothing yet. Just rolling, rolling, rolling.'

I understood his disappointment. I know Golden Boy will develop in his own time, but I too would like to see him with the other children, scrambling up to the story time organiser when she opens a book. That's probably why Mummy and I spend some of our time at home these days crawling around on our hands and knees in the hope that Golden Boy will copy us. In the meantime, I can take comfort in his other achievements.

'Wow, isn't he good at clapping? That's very advanced,' one of the mums commented the other day, which put a big smile on my face.

'He's been doing it for more than a month,' I said, not able to resist bigging up my child.

However, in two years' time these Baby Olympics will be inconsequential as all our children will be walking, talking, skipping, jumping, running, and doing the other things kids love to do. Some will be shy and some will be outgoing. Some will enjoy climbing trees while others will prefer snuggling under a blanket to read a book. In these very early days, it is almost impossible to tell how they will turn out.

Once they start racing around, destroying the house and doing everything we tell them not to, I'm sure us parents will long for the days when our children were harmless little babies. We'll probably wonder how they grew up so quickly, too.

Our baby house of horrors

Some might say that leaving a baby to entangle itself in a USB cable is an unsuitable activity. But in our house, it's quite normal. You see, we have yet to baby-proof our home, making it, some would say, a virtual death trap for our now very mobile nine-month-old son.

A mixture of our own laziness and disorganisation has left the place in a parlous state for our child. We have yet to install door locks on to the cupboards in our kitchen, behind which toxic chemicals and heavy bottomed pans lurk menacingly. The stacks of CD cases he is so fond of are piled perilously high on low-level shelves that he can access easily.

At least we don't have to worry about sticking covers over the electrical sockets, as they are all rammed full of frightening plugs, leaving in their wake miles of dangerous wires and cables which Golden Boy loves to yank and pull. About the only thing we *have* done is move a pot plant out of the living room ... after he nearly pulled it over. I must admit I was more worried about the mess he'd make than any danger he was in.

Still, having read all the guidelines on how to make our home a secure haven in which Golden Boy can play, I can't see how Mummy and I will ever make it happen. Some things, like attaching cupboard door locks, are obvious and simple to do. However, in a small London home, we just don't have enough room to take our hoard of books and CDs out of the living room and put them anywhere else. Neither do I want to hide *everything* just because our child can touch it.

Plus, what am I supposed to do with all these plugs and cables? We need them for things we use every day. All our so-called wireless world has done is create a raft of new devices, all of which need to be charged electrically. This means in our downstairs living space, the area where Golden Boy spends most of his day, we always have plugged in: a TV, a digibox, a DVD player, two lamps, a digital photo frame, two mobile phones, two laptops, a Blackberry, a wireless internet router, a radio, a set of iPod speakers, a still camera, a video camera, a baby monitor, and a cordless telephone base (I won't include the fridge, microwave, kettle, toaster, and baby food cooker as they all operate from plugs at counter height and are thus out of his reach). Just where and how am I supposed to hide the wires coming in and out of all these devices, never mind all those used to connect many of them together? Add on the Christmas tree we bought yesterday, which will soon be adorned with strings of lights, pointy stars and sharp glass baubles, and the area is basically a little house of baby horror, with doom and gloom lurking at every turn.

Of course, I am interested in protecting the safety and welfare of my son, but some of the suggestions that childcare experts recommend seem a bit extreme. While I'm happy to put covers on the sharp corners of every table we own, I'm not going to bother bolting the bookshelves to the wall (I couldn't pull them down, so I can't see how Golden Boy will). I'm not going to buy expensive covers for all the radiators – Mummy complains about how cold the house is all the time, when I think it's boiling, so I can't see how they can generate enough heat to do him any harm.

The fact is, children will get into things whether you want them to or not and, for a short while, parents have to be vigilant about keeping an eye on their little ones. Golden Boy managed to wedge his head under the sofa the other day. Am I supposed to put it into storage until he's eight and he can sit on it properly?

Until I sort out the things I can to make our little world a safer place (and it will be this week, I can assure you, Mummy), Golden Boy will continue to play our game where I say 'no', he turns to look at me, then turns back to whatever he is doing and carries on regardless. Cue floods of tears after I race across the room to pick him up before he hurts himself, ruining all his fun.

Holiday Fun

Daddy, I want a ...

Everyone tells me that next Christmas will be so much better because, by then, Golden Boy will be old enough to understand what's going on.

As he is just nine months old, the fact that I read him *The Night Before Christmas* and that Mummy and I sing carols while putting up decorations around the house hasn't really fazed him. Despite an interest in attacking most of the inanimate objects in our home, the sparkly Christmas tree that lights up a corner of our living room hasn't attracted a scintilla of interest from him. Even a braying donkey couldn't keep him awake during the nativity play performed last weekend at our local urban farm.

The Christmas parties he's invited to this week will simply be more strange gatherings he is forced to attend by his doting New Age Dad. I can look forward to Golden Boy crying his eyes out when he is placed on the knee of an older gentleman with a white beard and red suit and asked if he's been a good boy this year.

Yes, December 25 will be just another day for my son. As long as he gets fed, has a couple of naps, has his nappy changed a few times, and is given the requisite number of cuddles, he will be happy. In some ways, I'm grateful for all this. While it would be nice to see him actively engaged with the spirit of the season, I know that this will likely be the last Christmas for many years where I won't hear the words: 'Daddy, I want a (insert latest toy) for Christmas.'

The pressure put on parents to get the must-have Christmas gift for their child has clearly reached insane levels. It was reported last week that one lunatic parent splashed out more than £2,200 in an eBay auction for this year's hot video games console, the Nintendo Wii, which has a standard retail price of about £180.

While this might be the most expensive published example of parents gone mad at Christmas, I am certain there are cases of eager-to-please mums swapping kidneys for plush Igglepiggles (*the* soft toy for under-fives, I'm told) and dads promising to re-plumb someone's bathroom for Dora's laptop, another pre-school favourite.

Now, I love my kid but I'll be damned if I'll ever pay twelve times or more over the odds for something just because he's spent months on end mewling in my ear about how his life won't be worth living unless he gets it for Christmas. It would no doubt spark off an inordinate number of tears and tantrums, but in the long run, isn't that preferable to caving in to your child's every little whim no matter what the cost?

I'm not one of these depressives who thinks life is full of disap-pointments so my child might as well get used to them early on. I do believe, however, that in giving a child absolutely everything they want all the time, you are only making a rod for your own back and teaching them that if they moan loudly enough, you'll fix it for them. Not an ideal lesson for life. Even at Christmas, there needs to be a sense of reality.

So the Wii is wildly popular this year and there aren't enough to go around. If you are not able to acquire one by reasonable means for your little bundle of joy in time for Christmas, wouldn't it make more sense to try the following?

Put in an order for a Wii that will arrive in the New Year and write a note saying, 'I'm sorry, but due to a shortage of qualified elves in my workshop, I haven't been able to complete your order in time for Christmas. You have indeed been a good boy this year and will receive your Wii when we've dealt with our backlog. Apologies for the inconvenience, Santa.'

There may be some disgruntlement from your child at the fact the present will arrive late and that he's only getting a box of boring old Lego and ten million other things in place of the Wii, but in the end everyone will be happy and you won't feel you've failed completely as a parent. Plus, that phone call to your bank manager in the New Year won't seem quite so dreadful.

It may sound hackneyed in these credit-crunched, consumerist times, but the greatest gift we can give our children is our time. Fortunately, this year, that is all that Golden Boy expects of me.

'Tis the season of giving

'Twas the night before the night before Christmas and all through the house, not a creature was stirring … except for Golden Boy, who had a cough that sounded like he had smoked sixty Marlboros a day for the last fifty years.

It's not shaping up well for his first Noel, the angels might say.

All I wanted for Christmas was to see his two front teeth. But he's only cut the one tiny, razor-sharp tooth at the moment and, to make matters worse, both Golden Boy and I have fallen victim to that vicious cold that is doing the rounds at the moment. For the past few days his little head has been redder than Rudolph's nose as he's battled a 102-degree fever, his sinuses as stuffed as Santa's letterbox, and his chest more congested than the M25 on Christmas Eve. Meanwhile, I feel like I've been run over by a reindeer (not that it's concerned Mummy in the slightest). We even had to cancel Golden Boy's planned visit this week to see the mighty bearded one at the local children's centre, so unwell was my son. This lurgy certainly is doing its best to be the Grinch that stole Christmas.

Of course, through strength of will and copious gallons of Calpol, we will battle on and not let this dreaded ailment spoil our yuletide fun. However, with a busload of children and their parents expected to descend on our home today for some Christmas Eve cheer, Mummy and I face an awful dilemma. Do we tell them the full horror of Golden Boy's terrible cold beforehand or do we just pretend everything is hunky-dory?

You see, some things in life are black and white. You can't have turkey without stuffing and gravy; you can't have a nativity without Jesus and Mary; and you can't have Christmas without Elvis singing the hymns. Then there's that big grey area in the parenting world known as 'The Rules of Infection'.

There is a stigma placed on parents who bring their obviously unwell child, sneezing, coughing, and spluttering to social functions, only for their mite to pollute all the healthy children around him. Most mums and dads do the right thing and keep their bundles of germs locked away at home like little lepers so the other children can play in a virus-free environment. Still, there's always one parent who seems to have no qualms about putting the other babies' nascent immune systems at risk just so Junior can join in the fun – and nobody likes them. Therefore, would it not be even worse to invite the unsuspecting into a lair of fluey misery, where evil germs have been spread with every hack and wheeze, like a dusting of Christmas snow, through all four corners of the house?

Mummy, who has so far thwarted the virus, thinks not. While she has apparently warned most of our childrearing friends of the potential threat they and their offspring face when they come to scoff a few mince pies, I am not sure she has done it to the 'full radiation suits may be necessary' level that I think is appropriate.

You see, I fear the finger of guilt being pointed in my direction should some tiny tyke wake up Christmas morning to a head full of flu instead of a stocking loaded with goodies. I have already been blamed for infecting our little one (I believe it may have been passed on to me at work but I've yet to pinpoint the direct source of the outbreak). God only knows the wrath I'd face from other mums should their Christmas be spent tending to overbearing in-laws in one room and a wailing, phlegm-speckled toddler in another.

However, if a virus is doing the rounds like this one is, it seems to make sense that everyone will succumb to it in the end. I don't want to deny Golden Boy the chance to mingle with his mini-mates and have his picture taken a thousand times in his new Father Christmas outfit (courtesy of his grandparents – I may have poor taste, but this was a fate I hadn't planned to inflict on my child).

In this season of giving, I fear we'll be spreading more than just a little festive cheer.

I remember when the baby was actually quiet ...

I fondly remember those first six months. Golden Boy barely made a peep. I could count on my hand the number of times he cried. If he woke in the night, desperate for a feed, he only needed to make a couple of gurgling noises to rouse Mummy from her sleep.

Bedtime, in particular, was a breeze. We would stick him in his Grobag (like a sleeping bag with holes for the arms, designed so he can't kick his covers off or end up with them stuck over his head), kiss him on both cheeks, and lie him down in his cot. Sometimes he'd be asleep before we had a chance to leave the room.

Not anymore. No, those serene silent nights seem like a distant memory. Now a noisy nocturnal war is being waged in our household. The Battle of Bedtime has begun and it started the moment Golden Boy learnt how to cry.

It has taken him some effort to develop this skill. At first he would whimper and fuss for a few minutes after being put to bed before breaking into a full-blown wail. Mummy and I would look at each other confused. He had never done this before, so we would rush upstairs to find out what was the matter. I'd reach into the cot and lift him out for a cuddle but the game would quickly be up; Golden Boy would have a massive grin on his face seconds after I had plucked him off the mattress. He had our number but, unfortunately for him, we had his, too.

This resulted in the introduction of a strict regime of tough love. Determined not to have an overly clingy child who could beckon us with his every shriek and howl, we would ignore these false alarms, turning down the volume on the baby monitor and cranking up the sound on the TV. After a few minutes he'd give up the fight and be fast asleep.

Mummy and I may have won that battle but Golden Boy was still determined to win the war. He knew he had to up his game and realised that if he was going to feign distress in order to stay up a little longer he better make it look good. Now he's the Robert De Niro of crying – he puts in a convincing performance every time. He may only be ten months old but I give my son kudos for being bloody talented. His opening salvo is a sustained, ir-reconcilable aural assault that can last for well over five minutes (Mummy and I aren't so cruel that we let it go on for any longer) and probably gains the attentions of our neighbours three streets away. Upon going to check on him, Golden Boy will maintain this auditory onslaught for a few more minutes in the hope that we will remove him from the bedroom, that place where evil sleep-ing is performed. Every inch closer to the cot we stand means the cry increases in volume by another notch. Clearly he hopes we will take him downstairs to the lounge, where there is the excite-ment of television and the hope of staying up. To ensure we don't race him back to bed at the first sign of placation, Golden Boy is capable of instantly reverting back to his frenzied, screaming state, with the added effect of real, salty tears. These guarantee him more cuddles and buy him a few more precious minutes of consciousness.

This technique is virtually foolproof, especially if we have friends over. Golden Boy never wants to miss a social event and knows that any hint of 'tough love' will be frowned upon by our guests. Therefore, he's a regular fixture at dinner parties. Getting him to bed before he's practically fallen asleep in my arms is nigh on impossible.

The guile, connivance and downright duplicity of a determined baby can be shocking. My son has proved time and again that he will stop at nothing to get his own way, especially when it comes to staying awake. Denying him daytime naps to make him more tired at night has not dented his enthusiasm one bit; locking horns with Mummy and me at bedtime is becoming as much an amusing ritual for him as it is a wearisome exercise for us. The thing is, Golden Boy has the energy and desire to persevere while we're losing the will to live. He knows that eventually our defences will crumble and we will acquiesce to his demands. Still, as we are so desperate to be good, responsible parents who ensure our child gets his allotted beauty sleep, we won't surrender without a fight. I see a long and bumpy road ahead.

What will Golden Boy make of a 24-hour flight?

I have never seen my son as excited as he was in TGI Friday's in Heathrow's Terminal 3 the evening of our flight to New Zealand. He was literally vibrating with enthusiasm to the strains of Cher's 'If I Could Turn Back Time' while he inspected all the people in the restaurant and the gaudy Americana the eatery had stuck to its walls – flashing car indicator lights, photos of The Fonz and Elvis, and number plates from Utah.

Mummy and I were busy calorie-loading ahead of our first flight to Hong Kong. There were probably enough E-numbers, salt, sugar, and saturated fats in the meal we greedily consumed that we'd start growing ears on our backs but we didn't care. Nothing is worse than being stuck in a flying cigar tin for twelve hours, starving hungry with your only option being beef or chicken cooked to oblivion. Even TGI Friday's gruesome fare beats what the airlines had to offer.

Meanwhile, Golden Boy was experiencing sensory overload moments before hopping aboard his first ever flight. I was worried. London to Hong Kong was only the first leg. Another twelve-hour flight to Auckland was to follow. Could we possibly survive this ordeal?

Mummy and I had employed the same brilliant planning we had used when we decided to introduce Golden Boy to car travel. The very first time we strapped him into his car seat we took him from our London home to the west coast of Wales. It took us more than two hours just to get to the M4. By the time we had crossed the Severn Bridge he had had enough but there was still another one hundred or so miles to go. Believe me, it felt much longer.

Now, instead of taking him on a quick economy airline jaunt to Spain or France or somewhere else near enough to acquaint him with the rigours of flying, we decided to drag him nearly 12,000 miles to New Zealand so that he could see his grandparents. They were thrilled we were going for a visit but would he be as overjoyed actually making the trip?

'Calm' had been my watchword for the weeks before the flight. I wanted to make sure I didn't project any stress on to my child so that he, in turn, would not regale fellow passengers with all the vitriol his vocal chords could muster for the duration of the journey. It was difficult to keep my nerve when I was denied my usual pre-flight ritual: check in earlyish, go to a bar, drink heavily in the hope that the entire flight will pass by in a cosy blur and that I'll wake up just a little groggy at my final destination, surrounded by what I think is my own luggage. Mummy was having none of it. Boy, can the responsibilities of being a parent become a burden at times.

It was nice to board the plane first, the only benefit given to started kicking off as we taxied to the runway, my stomach began to knot. Never mind that long journey ahead - I was afraid I might be stuck in New Zealand for ever just for fear of making the return flight home.

Sleeping beauty makes for an ugly flight

The omens for the flight were bad from the start. I was told by the woman at the check-in desk that I would not be able to have a bassinet for my son. As my eyes bulged, my face turned puce and veins began popping out of my neck and forehead, she assuaged my panic by telling me we could have four seats across the middle of the plane instead.

Four seats. There were, in effect, only 2.5 of us, 2.3 even: Me, Mummy and Golden Boy. He's only ten months old - how much room could he possibly take up?

In my mind, I was already luxuriating in all of that extra space. The only time I have ever been able to really sleep (ie for more than just twenty minutes) on an aeroplane was when I had a whole centre row to myself on a flight from Montreal to London; I stretched out just after take off and had to be woken by flight staff right before we landed. Bliss.

I was imagining similar scenes on the first leg of our mega-journey to New Zealand via Hong Kong. Golden Boy would comfortably sleep on Mummy's bosom while my 6ft 3in frame got the kind of in-flight legroom it deserved. How funny that things never turn out the way you expect.

After a start-of-holiday gin and tonic and a surprisingly OK meal, I was ready to put down my head and soar away to the land of nod. But it seemed someone had beaten me to it. Unhappy at being constrained in the loving arms of his mother, Golden Boy insisted on extending his miniature limbs. With Mummy and me pushed to the aisle seats, my son starfished across the middle two, his tiny feet kicking my thigh if I dared encroach on his space. Despite being about one-eighth of my size, Golden Boy was enjoying double the room I was allotted. All hope I had of sleeping during the flight evaporated in that moment.

I envy people, such as Golden Boy, who can fall asleep virtually anywhere. It is a skill I have longed for but have been unable to develop. My inability in this area has increased my loathing of long-haul flights fifteen-fold. Unable to lie down, my capacity to sleep is almost non-existent. So while Golden Boy snatched a whole eight hours (eight hours!) of uninterrupted kip during the flight, I watched reruns of *Friends* and *The Simpsons* I had seen a thousand times and performed silly yoga poses in the aisle to try to get rid of the weird cramps in my leg muscles. While becoming more paranoid about developing DVT, I desperately attempted to avoid looking at that channel on the in-flight entertainment service that shows you how far you have travelled and how much longer you have to go.

By the time the first movie ended, I felt like I had been on the plane for a long, long time and that progress towards our destination *must* have been made. However, the map informed me that we were only over Western Siberia and that we had about ten more hours and five thousand miles left. What seemed like hours later I checked our progress again, but we had only moved two inches on the map. We were no closer to Ulan Bator than we were to Hong Kong. I began grinding my teeth.

Eventually, in a fit of pique, I took a page out of Golden Boy's book and threw a strop. Mummy rolled her eyes but plucked our child from the centre seats and let me lie down. A quarter of an hour later, I was told to sit up because we were landing.

Poor Mummy may have had to deal with two babies on the flight but my snatched fifteen minutes of sleep were worth it. Landing in Hong Kong was a relief ... there was only another twelve hours of flying to go.

Holidays aren't necessarily relaxing for baby

I'm beginning to feel a bit sorry for Golden Boy. While Mummy and I are enjoying a fun, relaxing holiday, I think he's finding the experience of being dragged across the world to New Zealand and thrust before dozens of strangers a little much.

The stress of all these new faces and places has made him a whole lot more prone to screaming fits than usual. Many of Golden Boy's antipodean relatives have been met with a gaze of bemusement and shrieks of horror should they dare try to cuddle him. Add on the facts that he developed a cough during the flights and he's got three new teeth coming through and the little fella has had a lot to contend with.

At home, Golden Boy has a happy and comfortable routine. On Thursdays, for example, he knows that after breakfast and a nap, we rush up to the library for Rhyme Time, where he will see the parents and babies he normally sees and is accustomed to.

After a few songs and a play with his mini-pals, we'll come

home again, where lunch will be waiting for him. Mummy and I then do our switchover. I go to work while she takes over the active parenting role, entertaining Golden Boy for the afternoon before dinner, thirty minutes in front of the TV for *In the Night Garden*, bath time, and then bed.

Now his cosy, predictable world has been shattered. After we arrived in Auckland, so distraught was he at the thought of a third flight, a mere thirty-five minute jaunt to New Plymouth, on the west coast of New Zealand's north island where his Nana and Grandad live, Golden Boy decided to treat Mummy to a golden shower while she was changing him at the airport before he went into full-blown meltdown.

We thought that once we arrived at Nana and Grandad's house and had our son safely ensconced in his surroundings that he would feel more confident to absorb all of these new experiences. Oh, how wrong were we. A tentative toe into the chilly Pacific Ocean received an icy reception, so instead we took Golden Boy to the local swimming baths, an impressive, modern facility that has three indoor pools and four outdoor pools to choose from.

I always imagined he would be a happy little water baby, like Mummy and I were. My mother loves to tell the story of how, when I was just six months, I leapt with glee into the pool the first time she took me swimming, smiling and blowing bubbles when she plucked me out of the water. Golden Boy has always been a big fan of bath time, so I thought he would transfer that same enthusiasm to a larger body of water.

To make the transition from bath to pool easier for him, we took him to the smallest, shallowest and warmest of the available pools. We sat in a quiet corner and lowered his little limbs into the water, all the while cheering and smiling at him in that idiotic way parents do when attempting to assuage any nervousness or fear their child might have. Despite our best attempts, the loud music blasting from the PA system and the nuisance of other children splashing around in the pool proved too much. He was soon sobbing away and clinging on to Mummy, refusing to even look at the water.

Mummy and I managed a couple of laps in the outdoor pool, to make the most of the occasion, but Golden Boy was happiest when he was rolling around on a blanket, shaded by a large pohutakawa tree, far from the water's edge. After much coaxing, a tiny inflatable paddling pool filled with just a few millimetres of water in the privacy of Nana and Grandad's garden is the closest he will get to swimming. After all Mummy and I have put him through, perhaps we should grateful he even likes that.

Nothing beats a grandparent's love

We took the jet boat up the muddy Mokau River to the fishing stand, where we hooked up the net that would eventually catch two flounder. While my brother-in-law Steve took off in his noisy, self-built speed machine, Mummy and I paddled back to the boat launch at the mouth of the river on kayaks.

Once the roar of the boat motor left us, I lay back in my kayak and let the gentle current take me down river. There was not a cloud in the sky and I had not a care in the world. I didn't have a clue what Golden Boy was up to and I wasn't worried either.

Let's give a cheer for grandparents. While Mummy and I spent a relaxing hour or so meandering down river to the sea, floating past ducks and gulls and inspecting the dense flora on the riverbank, our son was in the good care of his Nana and loving every minute of it.

It was a bit of a treat for us because, unfortunately, both sets of Golden Boy's grandparents live on opposite sides of the world. Mummy's family are based in New Zealand and mine are in Canada. While the distance from our London home means we can't pop round for tea at the drop of a hat, we still enjoy plenty of visits. We had all of Golden Boy's grandparents staying with us for a combined four months last year. It made for a busy and full house but the help and support they provided did actually make life easier.

From the moment they lock eyes on each other, there's an instant bond between grandparent and grandchild. There must have been something in his hard-wiring that told Golden Boy, when he was just a few days old, that he was being held by my dad. I could tell how at ease my son was being cradled in his Grandad's arms.

And how they spoil him! Between grandparents buying him clothes and toys and even big-ticket items such as pushchairs and high chairs, as well as all the gifts and loaned items we've received from friends that we again passed on to other new mums and dads (what I refer to as the 'parenting circle of love'), we've barely had to part with a penny for Golden Boy in his first year. More than presents, it's the time, patience, attention, and love that grandparents give that makes them so invaluable.

I often feel rushed off my feet when I have to change or feed my son while attempting to accomplish a number of other tasks; grandparents, however, operate at a slower, gentler pace that instantly puts babies at ease. I try to remember to be more like that when I'm with Golden Boy.

Still, despite the physical distance between them, my son and his grandparents do see a lot of each other. Through the miracle of the free-to-download computer program Skype, Golden Boy enjoys a video call from his grandparents almost every week. He especially loves to play peek-a-boo with his Canadian Gramma. It's quite funny to watch.

While on holiday here in New Zealand, Mummy and I have been keen to employ the grandparents so Golden Boy can play with them and we can have some time alone together. As any new parent will tell you, it doesn't happen that often. Mummy and I have got some terrific friends in London who do a great job of minding our son on the few occasions we do go out together, but there is something a bit special about knowing that Golden Boy's grandparents are taking care of him. It's the quality, not just the quantity, of time he spends with his grandparents that matters. Our trip to New Zealand has re-confirmed that notion. I better start saving for a trip back to Canada before the grandparents there get jealous.

Sometimes it's Dad who needs supervision

Being a part of Mummy's family means I have to participate in all the mad activities they enjoy doing. So, while on holiday in New Zealand, I've raced up rock and log strewn rivers at high speed in a jet boat (it took some explaining to my brother-in-law Steve that taking Golden Boy with us might not be a good idea) and I've scrambled, hundreds of feet underground, through mud-soaked caves with just a tiny headlamp for light and not a mention of devices such as safety ropes.

Even rain and gale-force winds won't put them off clambering down cliff-faces that have just the smallest of footholds, all covered by thick clumps of wild grasses, of which I am fiercely allergic. Yet, despite their attempts to frighten or even kill me off, I have survived – only to come a-cropper when walking along a beach.

After a long and lazy lunch at their rustic summerhouse on a cliff above the beaches of Mokau, on the west coast of the north island, I craved a little 'me time' and decided to investigate the seaside hamlet. Before I left on my expedition, I was charged with the responsibility of returning with ginger beer, the last of which had been consumed. So I slapped on the sun cream, donned my sunnies, slid on my flipflops, grabbed my wallet and headed down the road to town.

With only a museum (closed), a butcher's shop (closed), and two cafes to explore, it didn't take me long to tire of the village, so I searched for access to the beach, so that I could walk back to the *bach* (pronounced 'batch' and the term Kiwis use for a holiday cottage – not to be confused with the classical composer). Most places would have a sign directing you to the right route to the beach, but, being so laid back, the locals here haven't got around to putting one up. Eventually, however, I stumbled upon Beach Road and, rightly, it took me to the shore.

To access the beach, I would have to slide down 25ft of sandy slope. An easy feat, one might think, but one fraught with danger here, especially for a tender-footed person such as myself. The beaches are coated in black tar sands, which take on a scorching intensity during summer. Imagine the hot coals left at the bottom of a barbecue that's been smouldering for a couple of hours. Now imagine having to walk across it – yeah, not very pleasant at all.

I had been warned of this, but perhaps had not taken enough notice as I gingerly made my first steps down the slope. My feet quickly sunk into these hot sands, which seemed akin to molten lava. I howled in agony and sought refuge on a tiny clump of grass. I was stuck. My flipflops provided my feet with almost no protection against the fiery sands yet I still had another ten feet of slope and then twenty-five yards of baking beach to cross before I could reach the sea.

Absent of any intelligent plan, I decided to just go for it. Again my feet were quickly covered in burning sand. I had to run if I was to survive and rashly kicked off my flipflops as I made a mad dash for the cooling safety of the sea, all the while shouting 'My feet are on fire! My feet are on fire!'

With great relief I leapt into the surf, my useless footwear abandoned a good seventy feet behind me. It would be impossible to retrieve the flipflops without enduring immense pain and potentially irreparable foot damage (my soles were already lantern red). As there were no people nearby, I had no choice but to recruit help in the most embarrassing of ways.

I waded along the shore until I found the spot where the trail that led up to the *bach* began. Unable to reach the path by crossing an equally large stretch of searing-hot beach barefoot, I found a stick and began writing an SOS in the sea-cooled sands closest to the shore. Sucking up my pride, I wrote:

PLEASE
BRING
SHOES

BURNT FEET
LOST FLIPFLOPS

I turned and waved towards the *bach* and managed to attract some attention. As I could see the family stir into action, I added:

THANK YOU

Still, I did not feel this brief missive encapsulated my culpability in this debacle, so I made one further shameful admission:

YES, I AM A MUPPET

After a few minutes, Mummy's kindly brother Gary came to my rescue with a proper pair of shoes. He even went with me to collect my flipflops from the other end of the beach. But as I returned to the *bach* to be greeted with smiles and smirks and outright laughter, and asked to recount my tale, I was reminded of the purpose of my mission.

'Where's the ginger beer?' they asked.

Of course, I had none.

I am set to go flying in a light aircraft with Steve this week. I wonder if I should be more than a little worried. Or perhaps he should be.

Is there anything worse than parenting paranoia?

Firstly, Grandad accidentally shocked himself on an electric cattle fence on the way to the beach and then Golden Boy was almost washed out to sea.

The tide was on the way out so we felt it was safe to set down our towels about twenty feet from where the surf was coming in. I left Mummy and Golden Boy to play in the sand while I ventured out into New Zealand's rough, west coast waters.

As Golden Boy's new favourite pastime is to wave at people,

I turned around when I was about forty feet away, ankle-deep in the water and hollered over to my son. While we waved to each other, the water level kept rising to my knees and then my thighs. Finally, an almighty wave crashed into my back and raced towards the shore. Mummy plucked our son from the sand just as the sea rushed in, washing our belongings across the beach.

Mummy consoled Golden Boy, who was soon in floods of tears, while I raced about collecting sunglasses, hats, shirts, shorts, and almost all of our towels. (If anyone sees a green beach towel floating somewhere between New Zealand and Australia, please get in touch.)

We had just made the first pit stop on our three-day road trip from New Plymouth, home of Golden Boy's Kiwi grandparents, to Auckland, where we would catch our flight back to London, and we'd already suffered two near calamities. As bad luck seems to come in threes, I expected the worst and kept waiting for the third disaster to strike. But, somehow, it didn't.

I managed not to prang my brother-in-law's car during the journey, much to his relief. We even survived a trek through Auckland's congested motorways during rush hour on a Friday (imagine the M25 at the same time, but add on a few more road accidents – it was horrific).

Golden Boy was an excellent passenger all the way, give or take the odd cry of disgruntlement, and Mummy and I managed to 'cure' his fear of swimming (I think) when we took him in the warm and shallow mineral baths at our hotel in Rotorua.

Nor did he mind when a few over-friendly ducks gave his toes a nibble while we were enjoying a walk in pretty Hamarua Park, which is just outside the lakeside spa town.

It finally dawned on me, when we were settling down for the last night of our holiday, that I had been suffering an acute case of Parenting Paranoia. Normally I'm an optimist but after those scares early on in our adventure, I really was starting to believe that if it can go wrong, it will.

Paranoia is an easy state for parents to find themselves in. Babies and toddlers (Golden Boy now seems to be somewhere in between) – with few fears, fast-moving limbs, and inquisitive natures – bring out the symptoms. That's why I spent much of my holiday perched on the edges of the sundecks at the houses we visited (just in case my son accidentally crawled over), clearing things from the sides of tables (so he didn't yank them off), and generally attempting to find and clear any potential hazard he may or may not stumble across.

I discovered – right at the end of the holiday, of course – that if you spend all of your time worrying about what could happen to your child, you don't get much of a chance to relax and enjoy yourself. Sure it's good to be alert and aware (it only makes sense), but there is no point fretting about the unforeseen. Despite all the best intentions accidents still happen, so don't get worked up into a tizzy beforehand. Worrywarts never have fun.

When our flight back home was delayed, I told myself to take a chill pill. Yes, it would make our epic journey even longer and more hideous than it already was, especially for our active eleven-month-old, who is as good at playing quietly in an airline bassinet for hours on end as he is at reading legal depositions and completing sudoku puzzles while riding a unicycle.

Maybe he'll sleep the whole way, I thought, and then laughed.

There's a significant difference between paranoia and wishful thinking.

What I learned on my holiday

Holidays are a time of flux and change for parents and babies alike. Routines are flung out of the window, rules are bent and broken, and many a new thing is experienced, all to varying degrees of success.

Now that my family has finally recovered from jetlag and our various airline ailments (Golden Boy caught a cold during the flight home while I managed to contract tonsillitis), here are some useful nuggets of knowledge I gleaned during our trip to New Zealand.

- Always wear dark trousers while flying on an aeroplane. That way, when the baby is strapped to your lap for hours on end during a long bout of turbulence and you are unable to change him, it is not so noticeable when his nappy eventually leaks all over you.
- The baby will try to eat sand at any given opportunity and only discover afterwards that he does not like how it tastes.
- Like sweetcorn, sand looks exactly the same when it comes out the other end.
- They have never heard of the concept of 'child car seat' in Hong Kong.
- Having a baby as a passenger will not prevent a Hong Kong taxi driver from tailgating the car in front of him while travelling at ninety miles per hour.
- If Grandad one day engages the baby in a shouting match, the baby will often repeat that noisy conversation at full volume in public places, such as restaurants and aeroplanes.
- If all the adults present in the house think that someone else

is watching the baby, he will manage to crawl out of the living room, through the dining room, into the hallway, through the laundry room, and halfway across the concrete floor of the garage.

- Despite there being many more beautiful species of birds, the baby will be most fascinated by seagulls and pigeons.
- Corn on the cob doubles wonderfully as a teething ring.
- If a spoon covered in the sweetest, richest chocolate mousse known to man is left within arm's length of the baby, he will grab it, lick it clean, and look at you with an accusatory expression that reads, 'Why have you denied me this all my life?'
- Because the baby is not sleeping in his normal cot, he will invariably wake in the night and end up staying the remainder of it in your bed.
- You will feel tired most mornings because you have spent much of the night with a baby who has starfished in the middle of your bed, thus taking up all the room.
- Never, ever feed the baby kiwifruit if you are designated nappy changer in the forty-eight hours that follow.
- While the baby will remember nothing about your holiday, you will have many happy memories and hopefully many pictures and video clips you can use to blackmail and embarrass him later on in life.

CHAPTER FIVE

Growing Up

How hard is it to see a doctor?

Golden Boy is still waiting to have his eight-month check-up. He will be one year old in two weeks. It's not for want of trying to get him in. I rang the doctor's surgery a week or so after he turned eight months and asked the receptionist if I needed to book since we hadn't heard from them.

'No, don't worry,' she said, 'we'll send you a letter very soon informing you when to bring him in.'

'Fine,' I said, and hung up the phone. No such letter arrived.

Not that I have much faith in letters from the NHS stating times, dates, and locations of appointments that the medical powers-that-be want you to attend. Mummy received one on December 16 last year, dated December 15, informing her of a screening she was to have on December 14. It was the first she had heard of it. Big lot of help that letter was.

Anyway, Christmas came and went, and the New Year, too. We went on holiday and the notion of my son's routine eight-month check-up slipped my mind. So when we returned from New Zealand a couple of weeks ago, without that promised appointment booked in, I thought I'd better follow it up and rang our surgery again.

The receptionist, a different one this time, seemed perplexed by the notion of an eight-month examination for babies. I suppose training the people that deal with the public on routine medical matters is beyond the NHS.

'So you want, like, an appointment then?' she finally deduced. 'Do you want a health visitor to come round? I can send one out tomorrow. What time is good for you?'

A breakthrough! We could at last get this minor medical examination dealt with and my mind could be set at ease.

You see, Mummy isn't that bothered if Golden Boy sees a doctor or not. As far as she can tell (and as far as I can too), our son seems pretty normal. He can hear OK and see OK. He eats OK, sleeps OK, poops OK, is growing and developing OK ... doing all the things that babies normally do. Plus, taking Golden Boy to a doctor's surgery will simply put him at a greater risk of contracting some awful lurgy, Mummy says, as surgeries tend to be stuffed to the rafters with the great unwell.

Mummy makes a good argument. Still, I crave that official medical stamp of approval. I want a real doctor to confirm what we think is the case: that he's a normal and healthy baby boy. And if, God forbid, that isn't the case, I want to know about it straight away. Neither of us has spent the eight or so years training it takes to become a doctor. I want someone with that amount of education to give my son a good once over and reassure me that all is going swimmingly. Hell, it's partly what I pay taxes for. I want my money's worth.

77

Growing Up

going swimmingly. Hell, it's partly what I pay taxes for. I want my money's worth.

So when the receptionist announced that a health visitor – not quite a doctor but good enough – would come round, thus making life easier for us and preventing Golden Boy from being placed at risk of whatever viruses would be wafting through the doctor's surgery, I leapt at the opportunity.

'Yes, that would be super,' I told the receptionist, and arranged a time. The health visitor never arrived.

Just how difficult is it to obtain a baby's routine, scheduled health check in this country? My ordeal finally ended this morning when I managed to book an appointment with Golden Boy's GP, for nearly three weeks' time. It was the earliest date going, but what rigmarole. I know it's been a similar palaver for other parents trying to organise their children's eight-month check-up. It seems many doctors' surgeries just don't want to know.

If the NHS truly were interested in the health of our children, it would make these routine medical assessments more readily available to them. It's no wonder there are so many stories in the newspapers about children – and many other people – who would have had a better fighting chance at conquering their ailments if they had only been spotted sooner.

Is raising a child like training a dog?

I started noting down some of the things I say to my son most regularly and was disturbed by what they were. Sit. Stay. Good boy. Come here. No. Don't touch that. And it got

me to thinking, is raising a child in some ways like training a dog?

Now, this might seem a bit absurd or even demeaning to children but please hear me out. Of course, I do speak in complete sentences to Golden Boy and don't spend all day barking at him as if he were a golden retriever. I do consider him to be a person, an actual human being, and not a member of the canine species. However, I also think that, like many parents (and I've heard my friends and other mums and dads say the same things), I resort to these basic, dog trainer-like commands because these simple messages can be used to praise good behaviour and to instill some sort of obedience in a way that even a baby can understand.

Isn't that what we want from our children – for them to be happy and to do as they're told with minimum fuss? Whether or not that actually happens is another story. Anyway, here are a few examples of times when I sound more like Barbara Woodhouse, perhaps, than a parent.

At meal times, Golden Boy is great. Mummy and I are quite lucky that we have a son who loves his food and doesn't often complain when a spoonful of whatever puréed concoction we've come up with is thrust in front of him. So it's only natural to tell him, 'Good boy' as he wolfs down his porridge at breakfast or his vegetable medley at tea.

When he's exploring the house, of course we want to prevent him from injuring himself. Now you can babyproof your home so that opening even the hardest to reach cupboard is like trying to break into a bank vault but babies will still find something that's dangerous. Thus, when my son reaches the floor lamp that we've wedged behind a table and tries to pull it down, 'No' and 'Don't touch that' are the first things to leap from my mouth. The amazing thing is that, at nearly a year old now, he's beginning to take notice. Well, sometimes ... I usually have to remove him from the area to cries of disgruntlement.

Changing his nappy, however, is a different story. This simple procedure has never been easy, as Golden Boy seems to find it difficult to sit still for more than two seconds. But recently his antics have become an epic nuisance. And no matter what I say, he's not going to listen. His new favourite trick is to roll over and crawl off the second his dirty nappy has been removed, never mind what sort of mess may still be attached to him. Then he wants me to chase him as he crawls all over the living room. I fear the carpet will never look the same again.

This cat-and-mouse game, as endearing as it is, can prove annoying, especially as he starts bawling the second I pick him up and put him back on his changing mat. After that I can say 'Sit' and 'Stay' until I'm blue in the face but the words just don't work.

So my new nappy-changing technique involves me gently pinning Golden Boy's shoulders to the floor with my feet so he can't wriggle free while I quickly clean his undercarriage. As you can imagine, he doesn't like it too much. This position leaves me exposed in a crucial area and Golden Boy reaps his revenge by using his long legs to kick me in a way that will prevent him from ever having brothers and sisters. Saying 'No' when he starts booting me doesn't get much of a response either.

Like training a dog, raising a baby takes a lot of time and patience. Obviously, children are much more complex creatures than dogs and do require and deserve to be treated with greater reverence, care, and respect. However, when I'm chasing a dirty semi-naked child around the living room, telling him to 'Come here now,' I don't see much of a distinction between the two.

The good thing is, when Golden Boy gets a little bit older, I'm told he'll enjoy fetching me bottles of lager from the fridge. Small beer, perhaps, but it's something to look forward to.

Infiltrating the Mummy Clique

Since becoming a parent I've found that, in some ways, it is easier to make friends. Now when I meet a person, I no longer have to rely on finding out if they like the same films as me or have the same taste in music or support the same football club, the usual checklist of things most people use when deciding whether they share kinship with a person. Since I've been a dad, I've become immersed in this new world I'd rarely seen before – the Land of Parents. When I take Golden Boy out to the various play groups he attends, as long as he is in the proximity of another child the chances are I will become acquainted with that baby's mum or dad and, in many cases, eventually strike up a friendship.

Being parents with young children is a pretty big commonality and one that can provide hours of potential conversation. When you have a kid, there is no end of things to talk about – from sleeping and eating habits to growth and teething pains, all parents have been there and have an opinion on how to deal with it. And because new parents, for the most part, love to talk about their child and are often desperate to find out what other people's children are up to – so they can contrast and compare and usually come to the conclusion that their child is better – getting to know other parents is pretty easy. It's just a good thing that my partner isn't the jealous type because most of my newfound friends are mums.

Of course I know my fair share of dads. A group of us who met while attending an antenatal class with our WAGs still occasionally get let off our respective leashes to meet up for evenings of beer, curry, and merriment. However, as it is only mums in this country who get any significant kind of leave following the birth of their child and as it is mums who are most likely to scale down their careers for the first few years of their children's lives, it is mums who I meet most often. (Other countries, however, are much more on the side of men – my mate Malcolm, who lives in Denmark, enjoyed three months off from work on full pay when his daughter Isabel was nine months old because the year's parental leave that the government offers there can be split however the family likes. His wife had decided to go back to work. What a result!)

From Rhyme Time and baby massage to baby playgroup, I've carved out a nice little social life to keep me amused in the mornings I'm supposed to be watching Golden Boy. They say these activities are designed to stimulate infants and to awaken their senses. Really, they're set up for mums so that they can get out of the house and do something. It is only now, after several months of making regular appearances at these events that used to be the sole preserve of women and children, that I am slowly becoming accepted by the Mummy Cliques that dominate them.

I don't start work until the afternoon, so I take care of Golden Boy before lunch while Mummy slogs it out at the office. After months of hanging out with only Golden Boy to keep me company, I was looking for something to do to keep both of us entertained. I'm sure he was growing bored of me. I'd always thought of taking Golden Boy out to various activities, just like my mum did with my brother and me, but I imagined that he'd have to be much older – two or three years old – before he'd get much out of it. Then my friend Tania, whose then six-month-old daughter Lara was just six weeks older than Golden Boy, said they'd been having loads of fun at Rhyme Time, a half-hour of songs and stories at our local library. One Thursday morning, I bundled my son into the pushchair and took him up there to check it out.

I don't know who was more nervous when we arrived, Golden Boy or me. He seemed a bit overwhelmed by all the singing and clapping and running around. The children range in age from about five months to three years. I felt a bit strange and almost embarrassed at being the only bloke in a sea of mums and babies. Despite me not knowing the songs or all the hand movements that go with them, the mums were a bit leery but, on the whole, seemed OK about me being there. It helps having someone as cute and adorable as Golden Boy with you. He's the best icebreaker I could hope for.

As the weeks have gone by, I've come to terms with the fact that I look a bit silly when singing *The Wheels On The Bus* and *The Grand Old Duke Of York* and performing all the motions that go with them. However, because I've been willing to make a fool of myself week in week out, all for the benefit of my son, I think I've been accepted into the clique of regulars who always sit together and catch each others' children when they attempt to burst out of the singing circle to explore a foreign corner of the library.

Leanne, Jenny, and Toni have the swagger and confidence of the cool kids at school. They are such fixtures, along with their children, that they take on ambassadorial roles, welcoming new parents and their children who arrive as wide-eyed and nervous as Golden Boy and I once were. Strangely, I've started wearing the same brand of trainers, Converse All-Stars, as Jenny and Leanne. Perhaps I think it helps me to fit in. God knows. People do anything to be able to hang with the in-crowd.

Anyway, it's not easy to gain acceptance from the Mummy Clique, and many a New Age Dad falls by the wayside trying. Regular attendance helps; overfriendly dads who only show up every couple of months are viewed as plain creepy. And you have to make an effort while you are there; half-hearted singing and clapping or the inability to think of an animal quick enough for

will be met with tutting and a shake of the head. They don't have
much time for slackers either.

'So, do you work?' was one of the first questions I faced, again
and again, when I got to chatting with the mums after the singing session was over and the kids were all munching on fruit. All
of their husbands are at work, and apparently envious that I can
play and sing when they can't, so they couldn't understand how I
was able to attend a mid-morning activity and still provide for my
family. Explaining the unusual schedule of your typical journalist
took some doing but they seem to believe me when I tell them
that, in fact, I do have a job. The cosseted househusband doesn't
seem to be for them.

Similar rites of passage have greeted me at my regular baby
massage group and the baby playgroup Golden Boy and I attend
infrequently. I think for these mums it's just the shock of seeing
a man there at all. It is still spoken of as a bit of an anomaly. At
Baby Massage in particular, I feel I've been accepted just like at
Rhyme Time, as, um, one of the girls. The Mummy Cliques may
seem impenetrable but New Age Dads who are brave enough to
dare venture into their vicinity will discover that, in fact, they are
looking for a few good men who like a laugh and enjoy spending
time with their children. If nothing else, it does wonders for my
ego being told that I'm a great dad when I've done nothing more
than turn up.

Happy birthday, Golden Boy

My son is one year old. And I don't know what is more amazing: that he's survived a year with me or that I've survived a year with him.

Before Golden Boy emerged into the world at 11.15am precisely twelve months ago, I imagined that being a parent would make me look and feel more old and tired than I've ever been and give me more grey hairs than I already had. Somehow, it hasn't. And I don't know if that's because he's an especially good, easygoing baby or because, since I've become a parent, I've grown more resilient to stress and sleep deprivation – or because I let Mummy take the brunt of the burden. I'm sure Mummy will say it's that last reason ...

Anyway, I suppose having no choice but to deal immediately with whatever Golden Boy throws at me at any time of day – like his 4am teething fit last night – means I don't have much time to think about it, which is just as well. I don't know where thinking about it too much would get me. But there is one thing I do know. That somewhat hackneyed statement 'I can't imagine life without my child' is spot on. The childless may retch every time they hear it but parents the world over know it rings true. Personal freedom? The ability to do what you want how you want with whomever you want whenever you want? I can't imagine what that would be like anymore.

Many of my friends and family are surprised by how rapidly Golden Boy's first year has gone by and I have to agree. However, while the days have passed quickly, at the same time the date of his birth seems ages ago because so much has happened since then. To say that kids grow up fast is almost an understatement.

I remember cuddling Golden Boy for the first time, minutes after he was born. This tiny, bald creature swaddled in white hospital blankets, his eyes shut because they hadn't yet adjusted to the light outside the womb. I stroked his fingers, which seemed as small as matchsticks, and watched him in awe. He was so little, so fragile, so helpless.

Despite the parenting books I had read (well, the bits that Mummy had read to me), I really had no idea what was in store for me or for him. To watch the transformation from delicate newborn who can't even hold his own head up to the rough and tumble toddler he is becoming is not only amazing, but startling.

Golden Boy is now almost three times heavier than the day he was born. He has five teeth and a couple more are ready to burst through. He has so much hair he looks like a miniature surfer dude. He can clap his hands, point, and wave. He can recognise sounds, objects, people, and places. He tries to mimic some of the words I say. He has a personality. He can crawl around. He can feed himself, albeit messily. He's a master peek-a-booer. He can laugh and smile, pose for the camera, and entertain, all things he couldn't do 366 days ago (remember, it's been a leap year).

To accomplish so much in just his first year is truly incredible. No wonder people always say how amazing babies are. And yet we're still at the beginning. I know in the next twelve months I can look forward to him learning to walk and speaking his first words. However, like so many people have told me, I know I shouldn't look ahead to what's coming next but enjoy what's happening now, because once he's moved forward, there's no going back.

This birthday is just the first major milestone, both for Golden Boy, as a person, and for me, as a father. Of course, it's really all about him. I certainly can't take all of the credit. As much as I've encouraged him to crawl towards me or stuffed broccoli florets into his mouth, nature is taking care of things by itself. Much of my job was finished, in effect, twenty-one months ago. Still, I feel more than a little proud of how he's growing up. He will always be my Golden Boy, no matter what, and for that I'm grateful.

Happy birthday, my son, and many happy returns.

What do you mean another baby?

Now Golden Boy has finished celebrating his first birthday (not that he knows it – every day is a party for him), Mummy and I keep getting asked the same question. When are we having our next baby?

At first the query was greeted with wide-eyed surprise and a shrug of the shoulders (from both of us, I might add). It's not something we've discussed very much; having just the one to deal with has been enough for the time being. Now we get asked so often, we just roll our eyes and wait for the lecturing to begin.

'The last thing you want is a selfish, self-absorbed only child,' said one friend, a selfish, self-absorbed woman who was an only child and is also the mother of a selfish, self-absorbed only child. I suppose she knows what she's talking about.

Anyway, I don't see how being an only child is the lone criteria for being selfish and self-absorbed. I know many people – myself included – who have siblings and that hasn't stopped them from being self-centred in their thinking.

'Go for it now. Get it all over and done with as soon as possible.'

This nugget of wisdom is almost always exclusively offered by dads. I can see their point. The faster the whole hectic, stressful, tiring early months childrearing madness can be completed, the better. The thought of having to go through it again does sometimes send a shiver down my spine. Getting it out of the way sooner, rather than later, can make life easier. But that shouldn't be the sole reason for adopting an accelerated breeding programme. I also know of two mums who have become pregnant for the second time who tried to cajole a fellow mum to try for baby number two.

'Be pregnant with us,' they cried, like some rallying call for a bizarre reproductive cult. I think that might have put the non-pregnant mum off the idea of another child for good.

'Well, you don't want to wait too long before you try for another one.'

A charming one, this particular piece of advice. Yes, Mummy and I may no longer be love's young vision but I imagine our respective reproductive organs will function for a few more years yet, thank you very much.

Other people are less overt and merely insinuate that we'd be doing the wrong thing if we dared let Golden Boy be our only offspring.

'I couldn't let my son grow up alone,' said the mum of an eighteen-month-old who attends Rhyme Time with Golden Boy and me. She's six months pregnant. 'We didn't know if it would take a month, a year, or ten years before we had our next one so we started trying as soon as he was a year old.'

Which is fine for them. I'm happy their little family will be complete following the birth of their next child. However, I can't see Golden Boy growing up alone – there are such things as friends. I know they're not the same as a flesh-and-blood sibling but I can tell you that I got along much better with my boyhood chums than I ever did with my brother, Kevin. Fortunately now, as adults, we've found a friendship and civility that was wholly lacking during our adolescence.

Just because some people we know are starting to or have already moved on to their second child (although an almost equal number of our friends are stopping at one), that doesn't mean it's right for us. Really, I'm in two minds about having another baby.

Let's face it, it's a big decision. There are a lot of things to think about. One issue is child management. Mummy's only gone back to work part-time so she has more time to spend with Golden Boy. Will she have to give up work for good if we have another? My friend Caroline, who has two kids under three, says she's still trying to come to terms with the fact that her life now revolves around caring for her babies. Unlike a couple of decades ago, giving up work isn't necessarily an option or a desire for women (or men) these days. Everything is so damn expensive, you need two incomes coming in to keep up with all the constantly rising bills.

So if Mummy (or I - I don't want to rule out that possibility) surrenders her career, how are we going to afford another child? I know such an emotional decision shouldn't be dictated by finances, but kids ain't cheap. Of course, Number Two could be dressed in the finest hand-me-downs known to man, but he or she would still need to eat and have his or her bottom wrapped in innumerable nappies for the first couple of years. There are also hundreds of other incidentals that would need to be covered. Plus, as everyone keeps telling me, children only get more expensive as they get older. If we're working day and night just to keep a roof overhead and food on the table, when on earth are we ever going to find the time to spend with our children?

Now, this probably sounds like a lot of excuses and, if I'm honest, I suppose I *am* afraid of how much my life would change if I had a second child. At the moment we're managing just fine and can enjoy an acceptable work-life balance and I wouldn't want that to change. As I know from my first child, there's no going back once you have one. Deciding to have a baby, I'd argue, is equally as selfish as deciding not to have one.

The reason I think many people have another child is because babies grow up so quickly. Even though he's just one year old, Golden Boy has changed and developed so much he's totally unrecognisable from when he was born. I see old pictures of him and can't believe how small he used to be and how little hair he had. He's so much more mature and grown up since then, more mobile and verging on articulate. The change in him has been massive and it's happened so fast I can barely recall how he used to be. If I miss anything in his development, I know I'll never get the opportunity to see or experience it again.

The easiest way to give yourself a second chance and to provide a playmate for your existing child, make your family complete, all that – is to have another child. Plus, since no two siblings are the same (I know my brother and I may look similar but personality-wise we're chalk and cheese) then you get to see a different yet equally fascinating story unfurl over the years. Knowing what I already do about dealing with babies, that might make it easier the second time round. Friends who have moved on to child number two can't believe how much more smoothly things go.

So, strangely, that leaves me sitting on the fence. I'm armed with one year's worth of solid parenting knowledge, but don't know if I'll put it to the test again. I suppose it waits to be seen whether desire outweighs fears, so I'm not ruling out the possibility of another child, yet. To paraphrase the title of a James Bond film, I'd never say never. So watch this space.

Not the hospital again

The good thing about having Mummy's niece stay with us for a couple of months is that we have free, on-demand childminding. Mummy and I have been keen to make the most of it. The Au Pair may be another mouth to feed but she has a great rapport with my son and never quibbles when Golden Boy is dumped on her at the last minute while Mummy and I make a bid for freedom (she knows that, if she does argue, she'll be living on the street).

After a Saturday evening out with childless friends, however, Mummy and I weren't the ones who woke up feeling the worse for wear – it was an unusually sluggish Golden Boy. So we took him into bed with us for a cuddle to perk him up. First, I decided to slope off for a minute to make a cup of tea, but was loudly called back to the bedroom by Mummy before I had even made it down the stairs. Golden Boy had been sick all over Mummy, the duvet, and himself.

We had a sneaking suspicion this might happen. The day before, at the first birthday party he had attended, one set of parents decided to drag their daughter, who had been suffering from a tummy bug for three days, out of her sick bed and bring her along, 'because we didn't want her to be the only child not there'. I'm sure everyone appreciated that. We were getting texts from other parents soon after the party ended to say their children were already suffering from the dreaded lurgy.

So we suspected that was what had happened to Golden Boy and, as if to confirm our worries, he vomited again before we even had a chance to change his clothes. It was then, when Mummy and I were putting on clean outfits and changing the sheets and wiping sick off baby, bed, and ourselves, that the

Au Pair emerged from her bedroom to drop a bombshell on us. 'Oh, I forgot to tell you. He, uh, fell out of his cot last night.' What? 'Well, I had put him down for the night and went into the other room when I heard this big thud and I came back in to find him on his back on the floor. He cried for a little bit and I gave him a cuddle, but then he seemed OK, so I put him back in his cot and he went to sleep.'

Fantastic. I go out with Mummy for the first time in ages and look what happens. Before I could admonish the Au Pair for her negligence in the duty of care, Mummy instantly pointed the finger of blame at me. I had not yet put the cot base down to the lowest setting. We had it on the higher one so that it was easier to get our son in and out of the cot, but as he was getting bigger, it was becoming clear that we would have to lower the base so that calamities like Golden Boy climbing out of his cot didn't happen. I had intended to sort it out that weekend – honest! – but it seemed I had left it too late. Golden Boy was not even able to pull himself up to standing on Thursday, but by Saturday he was able to climb out of his cot. That's how quickly things change with babies. The accident that had occurred was all my fault. There was no getting away from it.

Mummy and I inspected the back of Golden Boy's head and it didn't appear to have bumps or bruises, nor did he on other parts of his body. But when he was sick again minutes after we dressed him in fresh clothes, I became more worried about him. I then did what I normally do when I fear for Golden Boy's health – I rang NHS Direct.

I quite like the NHS Direct service because, after I describe the symptoms to the nurse on the other end of the line – like I have before when Golden Boy had a fever, for example – they are usually able to put my mind at rest. The nurse that Sunday morning

almost managed that when she agreed that Golden Boy had probably just contracted that tummy bug that had been passed around
at the party and would most likely be fine in a couple of days.
She continued, 'However, vomiting is a sign of concussion and
if he fell out of his cot last night, it would be well worth getting
him checked out. Because their heads are the heaviest part of the
body, when babies fall out of their cots, they tend to land on their
heads.' I was already in enough trouble as it was, so I decided not
to tell Mummy that last fascinating tidbit.

Then the nurse asked me, 'Is the cot base on its lowest setting?' I had to admit shamefully that it wasn't and that I had
intended to put it down, but ...

'Don't worry,' she continued, interrupting my string of excuses. 'It happens a lot. It happened with my son, too.' I felt slightly
better knowing I was not alone in my failure to ensure my child's
safety – but only slightly.

Upon the nurse's advice, I insisted we headed to our local A&E
asap. Poor Golden Boy had stopped throwing up, thank goodness, but he was understandably grumpy and irritable when we
wheeled him into hospital. After we explained to the doctor who
examined our son what had happened, she too said not to worry
and that children climb out of their cots all the time. I was beginning to wonder if this was the stock response medical staff are
trained to say in these situations.

The doctor was fairly certain Golden Boy wasn't suffering
concussion, but wanted to keep him 'under observation' for
a few hours while she organised a 'consult' just to make sure.
We were moved to a gleaming new children's day ward and were
even given a private room while we waited for the consult to arrive. Several hours passed while Golden Boy sipped at water in
between naps and Mummy and I held whispered conversations
and watched TV. Unfortunately, they didn't have Sky Sports and

I wasn't allowed to nip out to the pub, so I had to pay a fiver to watch Chelsea lose the Carling Cup Final to Spurs on my mobile phone. Mummy wasn't too impressed when I found it difficult to drag myself away from the match once the doctor came back to check up on Golden Boy. She just didn't quite understand that it was the Cup Final!

When the consult finally arrived, we were itching to leave. Golden Boy appeared to be much better and hadn't been sick for hours, and not once since we arrived in hospital. Our case for early release was looking good until Golden Boy projectile vomited the peas and carrots Mummy had given him all over the place. It was like a scene from *The Exorcist*. Our hopes of going home were dashed.

After witnessing this the consult not only gave Mummy heck for feeding our child when he was clearly suffering from a dicky tummy – even though Golden Boy had been complaining that he was hungry – he also decided we needed to stay overnight and ordered that a bed be made ready on the children's ward upstairs. To err on the side of caution, he would see if he could organise a brain scan for Golden Boy, just to make sure he hadn't done himself any harm during his fall. Because babies rarely stay still long enough for an MRI to be completed, my son would need to be knocked out under general anaesthetic, which is not without its risks. The stakes had been raised much higher than we imagined. Mummy and I looked at each other stunned. We were certain then it was just a tummy bug, but the consult had instilled us with doubt. We faced a dilemma. Was an MRI scan and the potentially dangerous general anaesthetic that would go with it really necessary?

I was sent home to organise an overnight bag for Mummy and Golden Boy while they waited for a space to free up on the ward. The Au Pair was more than a little shocked when I told her that we'd have to stay overnight in hospital and that Golden Boy may need a brain scan but I reassured her that all of this was not her fault. These things happen all the time, I said. I was beginning to sound like a doctor.

When I got back to Mummy and Golden Boy, we were shifted upstairs. Even after our hospital experience in Wales, I had never seen a ward like it. I've been fortunate with my health and had not needed to spend much time in hospital before. I have broken my wrist and my collarbone on separate occasions, and had a brief stay when I required a small operation on my tonsils at the age of seventeen. Hospitals were quite foreign places to me. So I was shocked by the sight of all of the sickly children there – babies just weeks old hooked up to all manner of IVs and machines. While I was grateful that the doctors wanted to be sure my son was OK before discharging him, I felt like a fraud for bringing my relatively healthy child to this ward, to take up space and use up resources. Surely they could be better used on these other poor mites who really needed it. I may not be a medical expert but I was beginning to think that the consult had gone overboard with his recommendation for an MRI.

When we moved to Golden Boy's bedroom for the night, we were visited by the registrar, the most senior medic on the ward. We explained to him our fears about subjecting our son to a general anaesthetic and that, from what we could see, he was only really suffering from a tummy bug.

'So, what do you want to do?' he asked.

'Well, I'm not a doctor so I would kind of prefer if *you* told *us*,' I replied, all the while hoping he agreed with Mummy and me. If it was imperative to knock Golden Boy out for him to have an all-important MRI, then I would go for it. I just hoped this second opinion was contrary to the first.

Fortunately, the registrar agreed that Golden Boy didn't really need to stay there after all and that an MRI scan would probably be unnecessary. If his condition took a turn for the worse, we could just bring him back right away and go from there. For tonight, we were free. It was a huge relief for Mummy and me. The registrar then checked over a worn out Golden Boy once more, before turning his attention to our son's chart.

'Fell out of his cot, eh?' the registrar said. 'Now, do you have the cot bed on the lowest setting?'

'No,' I had to admit again. I was getting tired of this line of inquiry. I got the point. Bad Daddy! Bad Daddy!

'Yeah, my son did that. You've got to be careful with these things. But he was OK and I'm sure your son will be, too.' With that, the registrar sent us on our way.

I couldn't help thinking, are there any children out there who have not suffered this fate?

Fortunately, so far nothing has come of my son's fall from his cot. The tummy bug he had hung around for about a week before I got it, Mummy got it, and the Au Pair got it, albeit not as severely as Golden Boy. I fixed the cot straight away and it looks like it will be a while before he manages to climb out of there again. Now he just stands up and rattles the bars like a disgruntled prisoner when he wants to be released.

So what have I learned from this nerve-racking experience? Nothing is more important than good health and, if you are lucky enough to enjoy it, you should be thankful. Also, being proactive, rather than reactive, is best if you want to maintain your health and the health of those around you, especially your children.

Now, as for that stair gate ...

Making friends

To avoid having to attend eight separate birthday parties, all of the parents who met at our antenatal class decided to hold one big bash to celebrate the first year since our children's births. We hired the playroom at our local leisure centre and happily prepared for the ensuing mayhem.

With everyone wanting to appear like good, right-on parents, totally concerned with the development of their offspring, nutrition was high up on the show-off agenda. What occurred must have been a first. There was not one milligram of refined sugar in any of the snacks the parents brought. Never before had there been so much fresh fruit and so many fresh vegetables at a children's birthday party.

While the other babies were crawling and walking around, bouncing off the walls, patting each others' heads and pulling each other's hair, as babies do, our Golden Boy sat apart from them, crying and demanding cuddles from his Mummy, distraught at all the other children in the play area who were so obviously ruining his fun.

While Mummy and I often take our son out to 'socialise' with other children, he's never been a fan of babies and would prefer if they were not around. As he's never been placed in nursery, like almost all of his young friends, he's not been forced to deal with other children's foibles very much at all. It's not really a surprise that he doesn't like babies. Still, his obvious disdain to fellow rug rats is a little much and his almost instant adverse reaction to them is starting to grate. If they stumble and fall too closely to him, he'll cry. If they grab his leg inquisitively, he'll cry. Sometimes, if they even look at him, he'll burst into tears, demanding that the unruly creature be removed from his sight.

At times it seems we have the most anti-social baby on the planet.

Now, at twelve months, I know it is quite common for babies to become very clingy, particularly with their mothers. I often feel a little redundant these days when I pick up Golden Boy for a cuddle, only to have him practically leap out of my arms and into those of his mum. Also, from what I understand, children don't really begin to socialise properly until they're two years old.

While we can deal with Golden Boy's negative reactions to his contemporaries, it's not behaviour we want to indulge much longer. No, Mummy and I feel it is time, for the lack of a better phrase, to toughen him up and loosen the apron strings a bit. We feel he needs to be able to make it on his own in the rough and tumble baby world.

Part of the plan behind our recent holiday was to get Golden Boy accustomed to other children and we planned to do that by making the most of the hotel's top-class crèche facilities. Plus, by relieving ourselves of our son for a few hours here and there, Mummy and I might actually get to spend some time alone together (other than that hour or so we get most days, both knackered and slumped in front of the TV). It would be a win-win situation, wouldn't it?

We arrived at the so-called 'Kinderhotel' in Austria with high hopes. When we walked in, we could tell it meant baby business. There was padding covering the sharp edges of the wooden pillars that graced the lobby and gates that prevented small children from accessing the stairs. So far, so good.

The next morning, after breakfast, we headed to the 'krabbelraum', the nursery where children up to eighteen months were cared for. Everything seemed in order. There were good facilities, with only three other babies and two mature women, who genuinely appeared to like children, working there. It seemed we had struck gold. So, after crashing around with Golden Boy in the soft-play area to settle him in and then consulting with the staff, Mummy and I decided to leave him for half an hour just to see how he would get on.

With our son gleefully trying to rip the ears off a soft toy, we bid him goodbye and snuck towards the door, hoping for a quick and pain-free exit. As I was leaving, I turned back to take one last look at my boy, only to see his little face twist up and redden, his mouth open in preparation to emit the most blood-curdling howl.

This was going to be much harder than we thought.

Oh, wonderful day care

It's difficult to leave your child in the care of someone else when he's screaming the house down. However, if Mummy and I were going to get him accustomed to childcare, it was a seemingly cruel act that we would have to perpetrate. We slunk out of the crèche feeling a tremendous weight of guilt on our shoulders as Golden Boy's cries echoed loudly down the hall of the Austrian hotel in which we were staying.

We knew that once he had got over the fact we were gone he'd calm down and start bashing whatever toy was placed in front of him, as per usual. Plus, we were only planning to leave him for thirty minutes, hardly an eternity, so it wasn't like this was the end of the world or anything. Still, it was the first time Golden Boy had been left with 'strangers', ie not a friend or family member, so the whole experience was a bit of a worry. Would he really be fine?

'He was a good little boy, playing away,' said one of the childminders when we returned to retrieve Golden Boy half an hour later. He seemed OK to us, too, so we deemed the experiment a success and decided to drop him in there again for a longer stretch that evening while Mummy and I ate dinner.

What a lovely break! Mummy and I enjoyed some adult conversation and a proper, four-course meal without having to worry about our son attempting to throw everything within reach on to the floor. We sipped our wine and only occasionally glanced at the mobile phone the crèche had equipped us with, in case of emergency. It never rang.

After our meal, we headed up to the crèche to find our son snarling and cranky. We had picked him up a little later than anticipated, so relaxed were we about leaving him there, especially after a glass of wine or two. We put his behaviour down to over-tiredness. Once we got him back to our room, he was out like a light. No problem.

We were getting to like this whole childcare idea. Sure, we wanted to spend part of our holiday with our son, playing and splashing in the great kiddie pool the hotel had and so on, but to actually have some substantial time off from what can be the burden of childminding – even if he is our child – would be new to us and most welcome.

Without family nearby, we rarely get a break from the relentlessness of childrearing. Obviously, friends come round to watch him for a few hours every now and again, but it's hardly a regular occurrence. I hate to say it but I never realised what a relief not having to care for my son could be.

The following day, both Mummy and I headed off skiing for the afternoon. After writing out explicit instructions for the staff at the crèche on what and when to feed Golden Boy and discussing with them when he usually had his nap and whatnot, Mummy and I leapt aboard a bus and, with huge smiles on our faces, headed to the mountains. Schussing down the slopes through soft powder snow felt exhilarating and liberating. We hadn't experienced such freedom together in what seemed like ages. Trying to manage pretty much all the childcare our son has needed ourselves has meant we've rarely had moments out together.

No matter how well intentioned we had tried to be, with either one of us or both of us there for Golden Boy virtually 24/7 from the moment he was born, trying to balance that amount of parenting with both of our careers, our personal lives, and our many other commitments was taking its toll. We wanted to do it all, but this trip had proved something. You can't have everything you want without a little help. If we were ever to maintain our sanity and our relationship we would have to sort out a nursery place or a childminder for a couple of days a week. It was the only way forward.

We had always had a somewhat dim view of childcare and felt a certain smugness that we could manage to avoid having to put our Golden Boy in nursery. But the reality for us and for millions of modern parents, with ever-busier and more complicated lives to juggle, is that it's almost impossible to survive without it. Still, I don't think that makes parents feel any less guilty about it.

The hell that is a Bank Holiday

If there's one thing I know about living in London, it's not to go into the West End on a weekend or Bank Holiday. Those are the days when the streets are so clogged with people that getting around becomes a near impossibility.

Taking a small child into this melee of shoppers, tourists, pickpockets, trendy young people, vagrants, junkies, drunks, chuggers, muggers, and thieves is pure insanity. Most Londoners I know never venture to the West End if it can be helped. At weekends, they stay in their happy little boroughs, amble through their local shops and markets, sup pints of imported lager and large glasses of sauvignon blanc in their nearby pubs, and stroll through their neighbourhood parks and gardens. No urban-dweller wants the hassle of dealing with the hoards of humanity that descend on central London for hen nights, stag nights, shopping sprees, binge drinking, and bar fights, especially not after they've had to cope with crushing commutes all week.

So when Mummy said our friend Angela had suggested that both our little families go to the Aquarium, which is smack bang in the middle of the tourist zone on the South Bank, on a Monday, I thought great. Monday, after the morning rush, is always the best time to head into central London and about the only day I will agree to. And since, by surprise, I was somehow off work on the Monday she was suggesting, I was one hundred per cent behind the plan. We booked tickets for the Aquarium online so that we could fast track past the queues and I looked forward to our day out.

It was only later that I realised the Monday in question was on the Easter Bank Holiday weekend. I do shift work at the newspaper and hadn't really paid attention to Bank Holidays before. Besides Christmas, they hadn't meant much to me. If I work a holiday, as I often have to, I get another day in lieu. No big deal. So I never realised we were organising something on a Bank Holiday because I am not really concerned when they are. If I had known, I would have said, 'No way.' Going to the Aquarium on Easter Monday would be akin to entering a war zone. There would be bodies all over the place, carnage everywhere, and no guarantee that we'd get out alive. But we had already booked our heinously expensive tickets, so there was no backing out. I would have to break the habit of a lifetime (well, a working lifetime anyway).

It's not just London that makes Bank Holidays a time when we should all really just stay at home and potter around in the garden. Doing anything then is a complete rip-off and trying to get anywhere on a Bank Holiday weekend – what with airports heaving, trains cancelled or operating a rail-replacement service (if I had wanted to take a coach, I would have booked a coach and only paid the fare for a coach), and roadworks seemingly always in effect, despite the number of people looking to use the roads to try to get away – is a complete and utter nightmare. Who doesn't have a stuck-on-the-motorway story, with traffic at a standstill and a child wailing away in the backseat?

Even though we were only heading ten miles away from our home to central London, I was still prepared for the worst. From the off, things were not going as planned. Mummy, Golden Boy, and I had rushed around to sort ourselves out in the morning, raced to the Tube, and managed to arrive at our designated meeting point at 10.30am as scheduled, however, our friends had not yet arrived. We rang them, only to discover that they were still eating toast at a breakfast table way up in North London. Could we wait for them?

As a Londoner, there is nothing I hate more than tardiness. When trying to run an operation that requires military-like precision, such as taking a baby out for the day does, hanging around for a bunch of slowcoaches is not in the plan. By being late our friends had completed a tacit breech of our original agreement, so we would have to cleave them from our operation and fly solo. There was no time for stragglers. Mummy and I had precisely ninety minutes to see everything the Aquarium had to offer. By noon, Golden Boy would be too hungry to contemplate anything other than lunch, so if we weren't done with the giant fish tank by then, we would be in trouble. We had no choice but to bid our friends adieu, join the fast-track queue and prepare for a whistle-stop tour of the sharks and rays and whatnot.

Of course, there were the other battalions of parents and children running their equally important operations in tandem, so our progress was hindered by throngs of kids giddily racing through the Aquarium's halls and hogging the space in front of the tanks, with all their parents chasing after them carrying cameras, rucksacks, buggies, change bags, and all the other paraphernalia required to leave the house with a child. Actually getting to see the fish was a struggle, as was coping with the pushchair-unfriendly environment. Why are there so many stairs in public buildings? There are steps galore in the Aquarium that take visitors deeper and deeper underground, into the bowels of the old City Hall, and at every set I had to lug the giant child-ferrying contraption we own down them (the lightweight, collapsible pushchair we have gives me backache as I have to hunch over to push it, so I never use it). God knows how anyone in a wheelchair would ever cope.

Fortunately, at just one year old, Golden Boy's attention span is short, so we managed to escape the aquatic dungeon before it got too busy and before Golden Boy was hungry. We returned, blinking, to daylight and set off to accomplish the next task in our mission, The Search For Lunch. The pavement outside the Aquarium and the neighbouring London Eye was stuffed with tourists, who wandered around with their heads craned skywards as they attempted to take in the majestic views of the capital, but we managed to cut a swathe through them and headed to Wagamama, a Japanese-style noodle canteen near the South Bank centre. This restaurant chain is normally frequented by the young and trendy, so we thought that a couple of 'oldies' like us with a child in tow would easily get a table. Young people are rarely out of bed before noon on a Bank Holiday, never mind contemplating lunch. However, it seemed we were not the only hip parents with this brilliant plan. There was a massive queue of adults, children, and pushchairs outside the restaurant before its doors had even opened. How sad is that? At least Mummy and I could still consider ourselves somewhat cool – it appeared we had the latest accessory with us, and Golden Boy is a darn cute one.

Five minutes after they opened for lunch, the front of the restaurant was a parking lot for pushchairs, with the rest of the place looking like the monkey house at feeding time. Meanwhile, we had to stop Golden Boy from attempting to stab the very mature five-year-old girl seated beside us with chopsticks. She had a younger brother with her, so I can only assume she was accustomed to such antics.

I enjoy eating out with Golden Boy because it means someone else has to deal with the tornado-like destruction he reaps at the dinner table. With noodles strewn to the four corners of the eatery, we left and dug our SUV-sized pushchair out from underneath a mountain of compact, foldable buggies that had been piled on top of it. It helps that I'm thick-skinned, because I experience quite a lot of resentment from other parents when my non-collapsible tank of a pushchair takes up all of the space.

Mummy and I were wise to embark on our mission early in the day, as the queue outside Wagamama was nearly thirty-pushchairs deep when we left. The pavements on the South Bank were also rammed but we didn't mind, as we were ready to make our escape. With Golden Boy about to drop off in time for his afternoon siesta, we were passing by Tate Modern and thought, well, maybe we could stop for a quick coffee at the members lounge, while we're here.

We followed the crowds into the giant Turbine Hall and queued for the slowest lifts known to mankind. What really annoyed me was the vast numbers of able-bodied people wanting to use the lift. Why? What's wrong with the escalator? It's just as fast, if not faster, and besides it's only people in wheelchairs or with push-chairs that actually require the lift to get to another floor. It was a bun fight at the head of the queue, with all these non-push-chair people filling the lifts before I could get to them in time. Eventually, I bellowed, 'We were here first!' and used the push-chair's vast bulk to barge in front of a young family with small children and block them from a vacant lift. In the end, I didn't think the coffee was worth all the stress of getting it.

Fortunately, leaving the Tate was easier than getting in and we trooped over the Millennium Bridge and made for the Tube home. How we survived a Bank Holiday visit to central London without much incident, I don't know. However, I wouldn't like to push my luck again any time soon.

Could weaning actually be that easy?

Mummy knew it was time to wean Golden Boy completely when, after he had finished breastfeeding one morning, he smacked his lips, wiped his mouth with his sleeve, and issued a loud and satisfied 'Aaaahhhh.'

I agreed. It was time to put a halt to breastfeeding for good. We had wanted to wait until we came back from our holiday in Austria before we tried, just so life would be a bit easier while we were away, but the last thing we wanted was for him to end up like David Walliams's cringe-worthy Little Britain character who asks his mother for 'bitty' even as an adult. No, Golden Boy could now have regular old cow's milk out of a sippy cup like other children his age. His actions that morning demonstrated as much.

Golden Boy was twelve months old. Mummy had persevered through her full year, as recommended by childrearing experts, and had got him down to two feeds a day – one feed first thing in the morning and one last thing at night – although sometimes Golden Boy would wake up in the middle of the night and Mummy would indulge him with a top-up before sending him back to sleep. I was unaware of the regularity of these nocturnal feeds as I had become such a heavy sleeper I was inured to the hunger-fuelled murmurings coming from the cot. Mummy might be a soft touch but Golden Boy would have to scream blue murder if he was ever going to rouse my attentions in the middle of the night.

Now, it's fine and dandy deciding that Mummy stop breast-feeding but the question was, just how do you go about weaning? I mean, simply stopping is bound to cause some ructions of dis-content from Golden Boy. Mummy and I had already tried to get him accustomed to having cow's milk in the afternoon, following his nap, but he didn't seem that interested; he'd spit it out down his front and throw his cup on the floor. We needed a plan.

While I was at Baby Massage one Friday morning, I asked Saira, who runs the class and is also a breastfeeding advisor for our local council, what a good weaning strategy was. What she told me was a bit surprising.

'What your wife needs to do is sit your son down on her knee, look him in the eye – eye contact is very important – and tell him sternly that he can no longer have mummy's breast, that he is a big boy now and that the breastfeeding must stop. He is old enough now to understand,' she assured me. 'After that he should know that the breast is no longer available to him. But you have to make sure you don't go back after you've told him or there will be trouble.'

I didn't say anything at the time, but it was the most prepos-
terous thing I had ever heard. Who on earth reasons with a one-
year-old? Mummy was to tell him, 'Hey, no more boob for you,
mister,' and that was it? I couldn't see how this was going to work;
then again, I had no other idea of how to do it, so who was I to
say? Saira added that if Golden Boy did wake up in the night that it
would be me who would have to deal with him.

'That way he knows that he is not going to get fed. But keep a
cup of water for him by the cot in case he feels he does need something to drink. Anyway, he should be sleeping through at his age,'
she said. Ooh, a sly rebuke at our lax parenting. Again, I let it slide
and headed home.

I told Mummy this dubious advice but she was convinced we
should try it – mainly because it would be me, not her, who would
have to get up in the middle of the night, an act which I had not
done in some months. Well, it's not like I'm the owner of the boobs
of plenty. I'm not a fan of disturbed sleep, so I grunted at Mummy
and left it at that. It wasn't like I had to wean him from me.

That night I got elbowed in the ribs around three o'clock in the
morning. I heard Golden Boy demanding comfort and a little voice
whispering in my ear: 'You're on.'

'What? Did you have a little chat with him already? Did you
have your consultation?' I asked, as I picked up our mewling son
who was clearly unimpressed that it was me who had come to
fetch him.

'No, just give him some water or something,' Mummy
demanded, as Golden Boy's screams got louder.

'I don't have any water. I'm not ready for this. You didn't warn
me,' I complained.

'But it was your bloody idea.'

'Besides, you haven't had the consultation.'

Like with most things in life now, there needs to be a consultation period. Someone wants to build a big, awful high-rise building near you – they need to have a consultation. Your employer wants to make a round of redundancies – they need to do a consultation. Now, from my understanding, a consultation doesn't change the situation – the monstrosity will still be built and people will still lose their jobs – but there still needs to be a consultation first. It's just the way the world works.

The same goes for weaning. It may not be what Golden Boy wants to hear – that the boobs will from now on be off-limits – but he needs to be consulted before the decision is taken. It's only fair, I pleaded. We need to treat him with respect. As Mummy doesn't like arguing semantics in the middle of the night, she took Golden Boy from me and grudgingly hooked him up. The three of us were fast asleep again ten minutes later.

A few days passed and the subject of weaning didn't come up again, which was fine with me. I felt it was easier to maintain the status quo, to bury my head in the sand and to pretend that nothing was happening, that Golden Boy wasn't getting older and that it might not be so strange or embarrassing if he was three or four years old and still saying to Mummy, 'I'm hungry,' demanding snacks on tap when we were out doing the shopping or visiting friends. No one would bat an eye if Golden Boy crawled up on Mummy's lap and asked her to get them out for him. It's perfectly natural, right?

Then I woke up one morning and Mummy asked me, 'Have you noticed anything?'

As I cannot normally speak for the first hour after waking, noticing anything was really out of the question. So Mummy informed me.

'He's slept through for the past three nights. And I haven't been giving him anything before he goes to bed. And I haven't fed him this morning. He hasn't even asked for it.'

I was surprised by this turn of events. Everything had changed
so easily, so seemingly effortlessly. It appeared Mummy had
weaned our child without him putting up a fight and without me
even noticing. Golden Boy has accepted that milk from a cup is
the way forward. I wondered, why did we make such a big deal out
of weaning our son in the first place?

Parenting can, at times, be a difficult proposition and in my
case, being a realist/pessimist, I often expect the worst. That way,
when things go south, I'm not that bothered or surprised. When
something doesn't actually turn out to be that bad I'm more than
pleased and that was certainly the case with weaning.

It was like when I took him for his last set of jabs. We went to
see the mean Filipino nurse who seems to relish stabbing kids
with needles. I suppose, to be fair, if you spend most of your days
inoculating children you can get a bit blasé about it. I braced
myself for cries of agony and floods of tears. It never happened.
Golden Boy barely acknowledged when the first needle went in
and winced only slightly when he was jabbed in his other arm.
While we waited for ten or so minutes to see if he would have an
adverse reaction, he happily slapped the glass of the fish tank in
the waiting area, acting as if nothing had happened. It all passed
so easily I wondered why I had built it up so much in my mind
beforehand.

Golden Boy is nearly thirteen months old now, clearly aware of
what is going on around him, and much better at dealing with it.
Maybe I should give him some more credit for that.

Nursery nerves

We've done it. Mummy and I have set up a meeting with the head of the nursery that we think is best for our son. It's not too big, has a good educational philosophy, only serves nutritious food for lunch and snacks, and has lots of space, indoors and outdoors, in which the kids can play. A fastidious friend, who spent months researching all the crèches in our area, sends her daughter there and she says she loves it. That's probably the best endorsement of all. If it's good enough for her baby girl, it should be good enough for our son.

Very soon then, for two and a half days a week, Golden Boy will be playing with his peers and learning all number of things – good and bad – while Mummy and I will have more time to catch up on all the things we should be doing. Unfortunately that will probably entail work.

One issue we are most concerned about is the bedding-in process. How would we get our son to settle happily at the nursery? We need assurances that he will be content with the surroundings, the other children, and the care he will receive from the staff working there. We are not so paranoid that we want to spend hours each day monitoring the goings-on at the nursery via a webcam – a procedure that is becoming commonplace among parents in the US – but how can we tell that he's safe and enjoying himself?

'Oh, you'd be surprised by how quickly the children settle in here,' the head of the nursery told Mummy. 'It's usually the parents that have the hardest time getting used to it.'

Judging from our experience in Austria, I'd have to say she's probably right. After two short but seemingly successful stints in our hotel's crèche, Mummy and I had plumped to leave Golden Boy for the afternoon while we went skiing. We had a fantastic time on the slopes but by the end of the day Mummy was getting a bit worried about our son, who had never before faced such a time away from his parents. She was anxious to get back to ensure he was all right but, as luck would have it, our transfer from the slopes to the hotel was beset with problems and we were running late. I was more confident that Golden Boy would be all right and had to spend the twenty-minute trip back to the hotel trying to calm Mummy, who was making some rather colourful and unkind comments about the state of the Austrian transport system.

We arrived back just thirty minutes later than we had intended, but that was enough to have Mummy riled. To make matters worse, Golden Boy burst into tears and threw a big 'how dare you leave me here all afternoon!' tantrum the second Mummy walked through the door of the crèche. Mummy felt a massive sense of guilt at abandoning our son all afternoon long, despite assurances from the nursery staff that he had been fine, so she decided we couldn't possibly leave him in the crèche again while we enjoyed a quiet dinner in the restaurant, as we had done the previous evening. That night, we just smiled while Golden Boy tenderised the tablecloth with a fork and hurled bits of food at other diners.

Skiing together would be off limits for Mummy and me for the rest of the trip. For Mummy, leaving Golden Boy in the crèche for an extended period of time wasn't an option. However, I wasn't convinced – how is our son ever going to get accustomed to childcare if he never spends any time in nursery?

Of course, what makes it seem so awful is Golden Boy's tearful antics every time we drop him off and pick him up. The nursery nurse had said he was fine while he was there, so he couldn't possibly have bawled his eyes out every second we were away.

So it was while Mummy was out on the slopes a couple of days later that I put Golden Boy back in the infants' playroom for a few hours. Sure there were protestations from my son when I dropped him off but the staff were happy to see him again and quickly shoo-ed me away.

When I returned, my son was playing like he would at home. A fellow guest even told me he had seen Golden Boy enjoying himself with the other babies in the crèche that afternoon. Mummy was reluctant at first to believe this success story, but in the end acquiesced that we were probably more over-protective than we needed to be. It was more likely us making a big deal of it than him.

Putting Golden Boy into nursery for half of the working week will be the first step in the act of letting go. As he's just a year old, it seems like a strange thing to do. The headmistress was right when she said that it would take us longer to get used to the idea than him.

What do you mean the baby's not invited?

I was delighted to hear that my cousin Emma and her long-standing boyfriend Gary had decided to tie the knot. They seemed perfect for each other. Of course, from the minute they announced their engagement the whole family wanted to know when the big day was going to be, to which they replied they were still sorting it all out.

Finally, after several weeks, I received an email from Emma, who is based on the Isle of Man, asking me to keep April 12 free.

Mummy and I were really looking forward to it. Weddings, by their very nature, are joyous occasions and everyone likes a good party. Plus it would be a good chance to catch up with all the family. My cousin Carl, the bride's brother, lives in Chicago with his American wife Emily and their two children, Pearce, three, and Vivien, not quite one. We had yet to meet Vivien and they hadn't seen Golden Boy so the wedding would provide the perfect opportunity to bring the whole family together. Except it didn't quite work out that way. Carl called me a couple of weeks after the email had been sent to give me the news. There were to be no children at the wedding, neither the ceremony nor the reception.

I couldn't believe it. Mummy and I take Golden Boy everywhere. People are always accommodating. Even childless friends who are having a dinner party or just an informal get-together in the evening insist we bring along our son. We just tuck him up in bed in an adjacent room when he gets tired. Golden Boy is a major part of our lives. Mummy and I couldn't just leave him out of proceedings, especially at a big event like a family wedding. He's an important member of the family and only a baby. It's not like we can just leave him at home for the weekend with fifty quid and a mobile phone and tell him to call us in case anything happens. We have no one nearby we could leave him with. What on earth would we do with him?

Carl explained that his sister had mooted getting a childminder, but under no circumstances were there to be children at the wedding. Full stop. End of discussion.

This was outrageous, I thought. How can you have a wedding without children there? They all look so cute in their little smart suits and frilly dresses, running around being adorable. You can't have a wedding and not invite certain members of the family just because they happen to be young. Discrimination like that is simply obscene. This child ban just didn't make any sense to me.

The decision not to allow children to attend a wedding can seriously tear families apart. Not long ago, Billie Piper and Laurence Fox banned kids from their wedding. It reportedly drove a wedge between the Piper and Fox clans. Laurence's uncle, screen producer Robert Fox, a father of two, was said to be so put out by the ban that he boycotted the wedding altogether. Surely my cousin wasn't going to take such a severe course of action.

'No,' Carl said. 'But only Emily and I will be attending. The kids will be staying at home.'

It seemed reasonable to me. It's a heck of a journey from Chicago to the Isle of Man for an adult, never mind small children. Even in London, we are hardly close. We'd all have to fly over there, and that's not cheap. Then what are we going to do with Golden Boy when we arrive? Lock him in a hotel room with a stranger for the weekend only to fly him back home again? That would be no fun for him and would totally disrupt his routine. There's no way I'd do that to my son. Eager to jump on my high horse, I announced that I too was not going to take my son. Because we don't have anyone who we can leave our child with in London, I would be the lone representative from our household at the wedding. Mummy couldn't go. Being exceptionally considerate of others, she was more empathetic towards Emma and her fiancé.

'If that's what you want to do, fine,' Mummy said. 'But isn't it their wedding day and shouldn't they be allowed to do what they like?'

Yes, sure, Mummy had a point but I was adamant that the child ban was a poor decision. We're a small family; there should be exceptions made for my son and Carl's children. I was later explaining this fact to my colleague Anna, who's a big fan of Golden Boy, fully expecting her to back me to the hilt.

'I didn't allow any children at the ceremony or reception when I got married,' she said, 'and I think your cousin is right to do the same. Kids cry and fuss and whinge throughout the whole ceremony, they get bored. It's basically a day for adults. I didn't want to have any children ruining my day.'

What was she on about, ruining her day? Children are a delightful addition to any occasion. However, when my cousin Emma wrote to me to explain her decision to exclude children, I could kind of see her point. What with the number of children on our side of the family and her husband-to-be Gary's, if they allowed every invited parent to bring their sprogs there would be thirteen children under the age of three at the wedding, as well as many more slightly older than that. It would be impossible to accommodate everyone; it just wasn't feasible. She would provide childcare for us if we chose to bring Golden Boy along to the Isle of Man, which she hoped we would. Due to the sheer number, it was an understandable decision to make, but I stuck to my original position and told her that only I would be coming, still disappointed that her niece and nephew would not be there.

Some weeks later I had made my way to the Isle of Man and was seated with family members near the front of an old, stone church awaiting the arrival of the bride when I was struck by a noise that I never expected to hear that weekend: the cries of a baby. Someone on the groom's side, I might add, had smuggled their child in for the ceremony expressly against the ban. I couldn't believe they had made it past the ushers. Surely they were under strict instruction from my aunt and uncle not to allow such noisy beasts into this holy place on such a momentous day. They should have been ejected immediately. Needless to say, there were a few eyebrows raised in my section of the pews.

Anyway, the organ fired up and Emma made her way elegantly down the aisle, holding tightly to my uncle's arm, and we prepared for the ceremony. When the priest conducting the service made it to the point where anyone is meant to raise their objections to such a union taking place, the only noise to be heard was the babbling of a small child. I admit a tiny, smug curl grew from the corners of my lips as I stifled a snigger. No children, pah! But when the parent tried to quiet the child as they kept on making noise, instead of taking her from the church, I started to feel bad for my cousin Emma, as well as my aunt and uncle, Judy and Pip, who had worked so hard organising everything so they could make this once-in-a-lifetime event perfect. The child started making so much noise I could barely hear some of the vows as they were read and I was right near the front; it took the parents, who were seated near the back, ages to work out that removing the child from the church would be the decent thing to do.

Being the polite people my aunt and uncle are, little was made of the fact that these parents had defied the bride and groom's wishes by bringing along their baby and thus interrupting the ceremony. Still, the rest of the day went seamlessly (this child simply disappeared into the ether the minute the ceremony ended) and Emma and Gary have said they had a wonderful day. Really, that is all that matters.

In the end, the baby incident made me think perhaps children don't need to go everywhere with their parents. While we as parents may see our children as the centre of our universes, other people don't necessarily see them as the centre of theirs. When there is so much care and attention and money spent on making a wedding day go off without a hitch, not having children around probably makes it much more achievable.

Perhaps I was churlish for getting the hump at my child being barred and perhaps I should have taken him (and Mummy, of course) along anyway. With the help of a childminder, perhaps something amicable could have been sorted out. All I know is that I got the first lie-in I'd had in ages the morning after the wedding and, whatever the price, it was worth it.

My son's out-smarting me already

I've stumbled through this whole parenting business for about a year now in relative ignorance. OK, I've read a few things about what babies are supposed to do when and how they are meant to develop and whatnot, and I make a token effort to listen to Mummy when she reads out things from the many expert tomes she's studied. However, when I think about it, I've treated childrearing the same as I've done speeches at weddings and most of my exams at school – I've winged it, gone on instinct and hoped for the best.

I don't think I'm alone. I mean, how hard is it to deal with a baby anyway? All children do for the first few months is eat, poop, and sleep. You smile at them, stuff them full of food, change a few nappies, try to get them to react to you, and comfort them when they cry. It's hardly rocket science. It takes energy, patience, and dedication, things that cannot be learnt from books.

However, my son is no mere baby anymore. He's a one-year-old, a toddler who's developing at a pace with which I can barely keep up. His little mind is soaking up and processing information every waking second of the day. The intensity with which he examines people and events is frightening as he tries to glean every scintilla of knowledge he can from situations. Now he toddles around our house at ever-increasing speed and comes out with things that astonish me all the time.

Just this morning, before I headed out to my office shed at the foot of our garden, I turned to Golden Boy, waved, and said 'Bye-bye'. So he did the same, twisting his hand back and forth and whispering 'Bye-bye' in his cute little voice as I walked out of the back door. He wasn't just mimicking my actions. I could tell by the look in his eye that he really understood what was going on.

More annoyingly, one of his favourite activities is to poke the screen of our expensive new television, which means we rarely have it on when he's in the room (which is probably not a bad thing anyway). When he crawls over to it, pulls himself up on the stand, and starts jabbing the LCD screen with his index finger I tell him a stern 'No' and wag my finger at him in a scolding manner. It's never been that effective a method of correcting his behaviour, but I thought it might work eventually. How wrong I was. Now he simply turns around to wag his finger back at me, with a big cheeky grin on his face, before he turns back and continues prodding the flickering images in front of him. Cue a tantrum from Golden Boy when I finally get off my lazy backside and stop him from trying to wreck my prized possession.

Beyond repeating actions and things we say (his favourite words are 'bird' and 'book'), it's the level of understanding he clearly has that is impressive. It's made me realise that I need to be much more careful when I speak in front of him. Daddy's mouth might have needed washing out with soap on more occasions than I care to admit.

All this heightened awareness on Golden Boy's part is very exciting, but it has also revealed a complete lack of knowledge on mine. To keep up with his extraordinary development (a learned veterinarian I met recently told me that children between the ages of one and three accrue language skills eighteen times faster than people of any other age) I seriously need to up my game.

To parent properly at this level, I think it might be a good idea to know what I should be doing. Winging it, my typical *modus operandi*, will no longer cut it. It's time I start putting in more extra-curricular work not only so I can best benefit Golden Boy but also so I can get the most enjoyment out of being a parent.

As difficult, trying, and energy-sapping as being a dad can be, it is still supposed to be fun, and feeling confident in the knowledge of what you are doing can only make fatherhood more rewarding. So I pledge to myself, to my readers and, most importantly, to my son, to do what every good journalist should do – research my topic.

Who knows? I might actually learn something.

Laying down the law

My friend Malcolm, a fellow New Age Dad of a lovely three-year-old girl, Isabel, was staying with us last week and I could tell very quickly after his arrival that he thought I was a hopelessly over-permissive father.

I suppose it is obvious that my son has the run of the house. Just walk through the front door and the incredible mess speaks for itself. It is not merely toys that clutter our living space. Books and CDs Golden Boy has ripped from the shelves litter the floor, along with paperwork and other items he's managed to get his hands on. A drawer left open is, for my son, an invitation to empty it.

As a man who appreciates order – my grandmother's motto was, 'A place for everything and everything in its place' – I have struggled to come to terms with my son's overwhelming desire to cause chaos. And the amount of chaos he is capable of creating is staggering.

'What you need to do is set boundaries,' my friend suggested helpfully as I was picking up broccoli florets Golden Boy had thrown on the floor. When I put them back on the table and implored Golden Boy to eat them, he just chucked them across the kitchen again, only for me to fetch them like some obedient retriever.

'You see, when food is thrown on the floor in our house, that signals the end of meal time,' Malcolm said just a little too smugly. I was thinking of stuffing a few broccoli florets in his mouth just to shut him up.

Annoying as it is to admit, my mate is right. If I don't learn to put the shackles on some of Golden Boy's more violent impulses pretty soon, my thirteen-month-old son could soon end up being issued a baby ASBO. I'm sure the staff at my local library didn't appreciate the rushed restacking job I had to do the other day after Golden Boy ransacked a shelf of books, scattering forty-odd tomes everywhere in the space of seconds.

A few limitations on my son's exploratory nature would not be a bad thing. However, every time I manage to kerb Golden Boy's more maniacal instincts, he's back trying it on again a few minutes later. Poking the TV, ripping pages out of books, attempting to reset the messages on the answering machine – little escapes his grasp. Once he even managed to accidentally ring 999 after he discovered Mummy's mobile phone left unattended. I appear at times to wield little parental authority and Golden Boy isn't one for negotiation. So how am I supposed to reverse the current balance of power in my favour and quell Golden Boy's appetite for destruction?

Having been proven incapable of setting 'boundaries' effectively for Golden Boy, I rang parenting coach Sue Atkins, author of *Raising Happy Children for Dummies*, for some help. After just a few minutes, she was able to pinpoint the problem – me.

'You are your own worst enemy,' she said.

Apparently, what I have lacked is consistency. I may at first admonish Golden Boy for hurling peas around the room when he's supposed to be eating them, but I'll end up bursting into laughter when he happily persists in the face of my protests not to. So, obviously, I've made Golden Boy think he's a pretty funny chap, not

a miscreant with an unwelcome habit of redistributing vegetables
from his dinner plate.

'You have to choose key things you don't want him to do and be firm with him each and every time he tries to do them. You have to show him you mean business. He needs to know no means no,' Sue said. 'You'll want to create a balance but remember boundaries are there to protect him. They'll help him to learn and build confidence. You want to get it right now as you'll be setting patterns of behaviour for the long term.'

I've taken Sue's advice on board and am trying to be a bit stricter with Golden Boy. I haven't completely extinguished his ability to explore and cause mischief – the state of the house hasn't changed that much, I'm saddened to say – but he seems to appreciate the fact that Daddy doesn't like it much when more food makes it on to the floor than into his mouth. Golden Boy may have a few more boundaries to contend with but that hasn't stopped him from living on the edge.

Baby Talk, Baby Walk

Being a role model isn't an easy job

I was making Sunday dinner (a nice joint of lamb with green beans and roast potatoes) and was listening to 6-0-6, the football phone-in on BBC Radio 5Live, to keep me company. Ex-journeyman footballer Steve Claridge was hosting the show and making my blood boil as he kept defending the behaviour of Manchester United defender Rio Ferdinand, who 'accidentally' kicked a female steward in frustration after his team's loss to Chelsea on Saturday. He was said to be aiming for a brick wall when he 'brushed' the steward's leg by mistake. Yeah, those stewards just pop out of nowhere in those bright, fluorescent yellow coats, don't they Rio?

Caller after caller was ringing in to say that Ferdinand should be banned for his outlandish behaviour but the blinkered Claridge wouldn't have any of it, saying instead that the incident should be dropped because the steward who was assaulted is said to have accepted Ferdinand's apology. That's not the point, Steve. Apology accepted or not, Ferdinand is supposed to be a professional and, whether he likes it or not, he's looked up to as a role model by children.

The only way to stamp out (if you'll excuse the expression) this kind of behaviour in football is to make an example of the perpetrators by fining and banning them. Liverpool's Javier Mascherano was recently banned for an additional two matches after being sent off during a game for merely arguing with a referee. Surely booting a steward, accidentally or not, is worth more.

The ridiculousness of Claridge's flimsy defence reached its apotheosis when one caller stated that Ferdinand should be banned for life. Admittedly this was over the top but it was then that Claridge said that, with respect, the listener couldn't possibly understand because he had no idea of the 'pressure' professional footballers are under. Give me a break. Joe Bloggs knows just as much about pressure as any top-ranking footballer – they have to deal with similar stresses with their relationships and health as well as at home and work. On a bad day, a hospital ward, classroom, mechanics yard, office, or driver's seat of a bus can all be as pressurised an environment as a football stadium. And a look at the current state of the economy will show that, compared with most footballers – Steve Claridge states on his MySpace page that his income is '£250,000 and higher' – your average person is certainly feeling far more fiscal pressure these days.

What about all those low-income people who will get financially hammered after the abolition of the 10p tax? How outrageous. Struggling to survive on an even smaller low-wage salary in a credit-crunched economy – now that's what I call pressure.

Plus, some millionaires probably don't pay much or any tax on their grotesque wealth, as many of them have non-domicile status and avoid stumping up their fair share for the public coffers to the tune of some £126 billion a year, according to some reports. Yeah, let all the bankers who get paid millions for screwing up the economy get off tax-free while the lowest earners pay for the upkeep of the nation's crumbling infrastructure. Nice one.

Anyway, as you can see, I was building myself into a nice little frenzy while Claridge twittered on and I found myself yelling at the radio, as one does, using the kind of colourful language that is apparently popular with truckers and sailors. I went into the living room – not that I needed to travel that far to have my feelings heard – and regaled Mummy with my views of this obscene situation. I was well into my stride when Mummy cut me off abruptly and pointed to Golden Boy, who had stopped crawling across the carpet and was watching me wide-eyed. He appeared at that moment, I am saddened to say, almost a little scared of his dad. 'Why on earth is Daddy yelling and looking so angry?' his expression seemed to say. Of course, I felt guilty and went over to him right away to make amends. After a cuddle and a bit of a play, he seemed to have accepted what I guess was my apology.

It's easy to forget that our children are there when we get lost in our own worlds, but they see and pick up on every little thing we do, even when they are as young as my son. I suppose I am used to having a rant when discussing events with my friends or my colleagues, but perhaps I, like Rio Ferdinand, should learn to keep my emotions in check sometimes. I, too, am a role model and shouldn't forget my responsibilities.

At the beginning of *Ham on Rye*, the semi-autobiographic tale of writer Charles Bukowski's childhood and adolescence, his literary alter-ego Henry Chinaski says that from an early age his father seemed like an angry man and that he never liked him because of it. I am not the cruel and brutal father Bukowski had, but I would hate for Golden Boy to grow up and ever say that of me.

Daddies were made to be beaten

I was looking at myself in the mirror the other morning before shaving and noticed I had two great scabs on the side of my nose and a huge scratch down my left cheek – and I had not even put a razor to my skin yet. The cause of this damage to my face? Oh, I had just been playing with my son.

Golden Boy can be one vicious little bugger. Frighteningly, he can be downright sadistic, too. At times he just loves causing pain and reaping damage. However, he doesn't perform random assaults on adults or other babies he meets. For them he's as sweet as pie and everyone I know can't imagine that he would ever hurt a fly. No, these violent tendencies are mostly reserved for one person and one person alone and that's me.

Play-fighting with Daddy is quickly becoming a blood sport, with the person getting hurt being yours truly. This morning I had Golden Boy pinned to the ground and was tickling him and growling at him, which he loves. He was shrieking with laughter before he crawled away from my grasp. I rolled over and lay on my back and, before I could move out of the way, Golden Boy had grabbed a CD case that had been left on a shelf and whacked me in the face with it. He stabbed me with one of the sharp corners, right on the chin.

'Ow, you little maniac,' I yelled, clutching my face as Golden Boy started guffawing. 'That's not funny. We don't do this.'

Before I could tell him off further he had hooked his little fingers into my nostrils and was attempting to lift up my head by my nose. I yelled out again and he soon let go. I rolled over to look at my son and he had the biggest smile plastered across his face. Making Daddy wince in pain was fun for him. I knew then that our roughhousing had gone too far. I would have to quash this kind of violent behaviour before it got even more out of hand and I ended up in a full body cast or worse. However, I had other, more pressing issues to deal with first. I had wiped my nose and found it was bleeding.

Now, I've tried to discover the root cause of all this aggression that Golden Boy is exhibiting. Normally he's really a rather lovely boy and, sometimes, totally indiscriminate with his affection. The other day, when out with Mummy, he was blowing kisses from his pushchair to the drunks in Victoria Park in Hackney; this morning he was gifting kisses to the pigeons across the green. He'll often say 'cuddle' when I pick him up and then bury his head in my shoulder. Then I'll ask, 'Have you got a kiss for Daddy?' And this wet, semi-open mouth will move slowly towards mine for some kind of contact, but without the pucker from his side. He hasn't quite figured that out yet. Then he'll hold on to me lovingly for a while longer, before sinking his teeth into my shoulder.

In trying to deduce the reasons for this behaviour, I've gone back almost eight months to when Golden Boy was only half a year old. It was then that he started to come into himself as a person and when he began to be robust enough to handle a little tickling and to have me blow on his tummy or on his neck so that it would make a rude noise. From the start, my son loved this and he would usually try to join in the fun by grabbing my ears and seeing how far he could pull them from my head. Then he insisted in sticking his fingers into my mouth, whereby I'd pretend to bite them. Golden Boy thought this was hilarious, so I'd bite his arm ever so gently – never leaving marks or anything ridiculous, mind – and it would have him roaring with laughter. I suppose I can only blame myself when he thinks it's OK to sink his teeth into my shoulder or, as he did the other day, walk up behind Mummy and bite into the back of her thigh just above her knee.

Now, if he did this to anyone other than the two of us, I'd be worried. However, the savagery is restricted to just his parents and mainly to me, so I'm guessing it's a case of him becoming too excited at times, getting a bit carried away and not quite understanding his own strength or just how sharp his teeth are (there is nothing more strange than the sight of six tiny teeth coming to attack your nose and few things more painful). More than that, he's trying to express his affection for us. It brings new meaning to the saying 'love hurts'. So the million pound question is, how do I temper his zealousness while not stopping the roughhousing all together?

The thing is, it's fun and I like it too, when he's not tearing great lumps of flesh off me. When he was learning to crawl, all I had to do was lie down across the living room floor and I had him entertained for a good twenty minutes as he kept crawling all over my chest. Now he likes to body slam me and try to stand up afterwards by pushing down on my windpipe – purely by accident, of course. I'm sure his knowledge of human physiology is not that great.

That said, at the rate he's going and with the moves he's developing, I'm sure a lucrative career in professional wrestling awaits. Just the kind of job every parent dreams of for their child ...

Mummy seems to be the hardest word

I woke up this morning to two wonderful words, 'Daddy, cuddle.'

Golden Boy was standing up in his cot with his arms out-stretched towards me and he had a big smile on his face as he said the word 'cuddle' again in that cute little voice of his. Life doesn't get much better than that.

I've been amazed by how quickly my son is learning to speak. He's only thirteen months old but already his vocabulary has stretched to about fifty words and is increasing all the time. As well as Daddy, he can say book, ball, bird, door, bowl, cup, spoon, bath, flower, shower, down, and outside – and many more. We bought him a book of baby's first words and he had the dozen or so words down pat in a day. Even difficult words like strawberry. He can also say butterfly, although it comes out as 'butt fly'.

He also says words and phrases that he probably shouldn't, such as 'fart pants' (one of his innumerable nicknames – he is quite a windy child) and 'boobies'. They sound so funny when they come out of his mouth that Mummy and I let him say them against our better judgment. I suppose our low standards in this department will come back to haunt us later.

However, there is one word that Golden Boy either cannot or simply will not say (it's difficult to tell which) and it is causing a fair bit of upset in our household. That word is 'Mummy'.

As you can imagine, my partner is having some difficulty accepting this. While Golden Boy will happily point at me and say 'Daddy' or a tree and say 'tree' or a computer and say 'puter', he won't do the same with his mother. At best she'll get 'Hi' or 'cuddle'. On rare occasions he'll say 'Mama', whispered very quietly, usually before he bites her shoulder. However, more often than not he'll call her 'Daddy'. That doesn't go down too well with his mum. It goes down even worse if I have to stifle a smirk and a giggle after he does it. Apparently, that's not helping things, so Mummy says ...

Anyway, we cannot fathom why he won't say 'Mummy'. Maybe he thinks it's a funny game and he enjoys having a cruel laugh at his mum's expense. If the lad can get his head around other objects and creatures and can put a name to them, he should be able to do the same with his Mummy. It is not that hard to say and it is one of the first words a baby is supposed to utter. His reluctance to say the word doesn't make any sense. However, logic doesn't always enter the equation when it comes to childrearing.

Here's an example. The other day the three of us were out shopping. While I thought it could be a nice day out, with a good lunch stop in the middle, it turned out to be a long, drawn out experience and one that I would not recommend be attempted too frequently. Neither would the staff at the various shops we visited, who were either greeted by a child screaming because he was strapped into his pushchair or a mountain of clothes to be refolded after said child was released from his pushchair so that he could explore. Going shopping alone is quicker, more efficient, and easier for everyone involved.

I was guiding Golden Boy's pushchair through a women's clothing store while Mummy looked for a new frock when I spied something that appeared right for her. So, in an attempt to be useful, I picked the dress from the rack and called out to Mummy, who was about ten feet away.

'Di! What do you think of this?' I said, holding the dress aloft for her inspection. Before she could comment on the stripy garment, which she didn't like anyway, a little voice let us know that he had picked up on something new.

'Di,' Golden Boy said, looking at Mummy. 'Di, Di, Di, Di, Di, Di.'

I think you can see where this is going. 'Di' became the only word my son would say for the rest of the day, much to the annoyance of Di, who would prefer that her son addressed her as Mummy and not by the abbreviated form of her Christian name, Dianne. Of course, all of this was my fault.

'You were the one who kept saying my name all the time,' she claimed.

Well, what else am I supposed to call her? I guess this is why couples that are parents almost always refer to each other 'mummy' and 'daddy'.

Since this incident, Golden Boy seems to have put his mum's name out of his mind and prefers to call her 'Daddy' when prompted or just babble away in his incomprehensible baby talk. Perhaps he has invented a nickname for Mummy that we are yet to pick up on. At least he hasn't called her 'fart pants'.

As Golden Boy's language skills continue to develop at an unbelievably rapid rate, Mummy still seems to be the hardest word.

Some things should be done by the book

Golden Boy's ability to speak, at just thirteen and a half months old, impresses everyone he knows. 'That's really early,' said my friend Jenny the other day, when I told her of my son's linguistic accomplishment. She's an early years

educator, so she should know. The women at his nursery are amazed that he's learned all their names in a matter of days. 'He's very advanced,' said Grace, who runs the Montessori that Golden Boy attends. Even better was the accolade my friend Kirsty awarded Golden Boy after she had watched him for a few hours last week.

'He's a genius,' she said. 'I've never heard a baby that young speak before.'

Well, Kirsty might be over-egging it a bit, but all this praise for Golden Boy does swell my heart with pride and put a beatific smile on my face. It was what she said next that, for me, really hits the nail on the head.

'Wow, all that reading you do must really work.'

The only thing I know for sure that I've got right as a parent is that I started reading to Golden Boy from early on. This, I would say, is the reason for his budding language skills.

If I'm a zealot about any childhood issue it's literacy. A quick look at the statistics on literacy in this country make for, well, grim reading. There seems to be a new report out every day be-moaning the lack of grammar and reading ability in children. It's been reported that nearly one in five children leaves school fundamentally illiterate. Not only is this a shocking example of how our education system is failing, it's also an example of how we as parents are failing our children.

Then again, adults in this country don't seem to be much better. A study I read yesterday revealed that two-thirds of adults in Britain have the reading ability of an eleven-year-old; many can barely understand the lyrics that run across the screen at karaoke. This in an era when there are more published words than ever before. I find it all very saddening because so many people don't know what they're missing. The joys of reading are many and I'm glad I've been able to pass them down to my son from an early age.

I started reading to Golden Boy when he was only a few months old. Basically, I was at a loss for ways to connect with my son. At three or four months, he didn't really do much but I knew I could lie down on my bed with him before his nap and read a few stories before he got bored or drifted off to sleep. My mum had always read to me as a child, so I suppose I took this from her and carried on the legacy.

I knew that Golden Boy wouldn't understand what I was saying but he listened anyway and seemed to enjoy the pictures in books such as *The Gruffalo* and *The Very Hungry Caterpillar*. The books with rhymes, such as *The Owl and The Pussycat*, seemed to be the stories he enjoyed most, as he could listen to the rhythm of the words.

Soon, his attention span grew and he would want to read up to five or six books before having his nap. Now, he's a total book freak. He brings them over to me to read to him at all hours of the day, sometimes wanting me to read a dozen books at a sitting, demanding 'more, more, more'. He likes to play and run around and explore, like most children his age, but already it's apparent that he wants reading to be a big part of his life. It's no surprise that his first word – and one of the words I now hear most often – was 'book'.

While I knew reading to Golden Boy would be beneficial, I mostly started doing it because it was fun. Golden Boy likes pointing out the different animals and mimicking their sounds in *Brown Bear, Brown Bear, What Can You See?* His goldfish impersonation is hilarious, as he sucks in his cheeks and makes a popping sound with his mouth. He now gets so excited on the penultimate page of *The Very Hungry Caterpillar*, knowing, since we've read it about ten thousand times, that the creature about to emerge from his cocoon will become a beautiful butterfly on the last page.

When he loses interest in the book we're looking at, I leave him be. Reading now is totally on his accord. I don't want to be overzealous and 'hot-house' him, and I certainly don't expect him to be reciting Shakespeare on his second birthday or anything silly like that. What would be the point? I wouldn't want to make books and reading seem arduous to him and kill his enjoyment of them completely.

Still, I'm glad I am giving him a head start. A new study has shown that reading to children from an early age promotes their motor skills (through learning to turn the pages) and their memories, as well as their emotional and social development. Professor Barry Zuckerman of Boston University who led the study said that reading aloud between a parent and child reinforces it as a pleasurable activity.

'Children ultimately learn to love books because they are sharing it with someone they love,' he said. What better way to spend time can there be?

I know in this world of interactive television and multimedia extravaganzas that books must seem old, dull, boring, and stuffy. However, they are equally a gateway to the imagination and provide the escape that everyone craves. I know I may have more of a battle on my hands as Golden Boy gets older and becomes interested in video games and the Internet, but I hope that I've started a literary love affair that will last him a lifetime. At the moment, it seems to be getting better all the time.

One small step for man, one giant leap for Golden Boy

My son can walk. It's pretty amazing. When he really started going for it the other day, I was almost late for work because I couldn't stop watching him. Mummy and I sat at either end of the hallway upstairs in our house and our son walked from one of us to the other. He looked something like a cross between a robot and an ape. His arms were held aloft just like Clyde the orangutan in that dreadful but somehow watchable film *Every Which Way but Loose* **that Clint Eastwood did in the late Seventies, while his legs were almost rigid, his knees locked in place. He staggered a bit like a drunk as he weaved his imperfect path from Mummy to me and then fell into my arms with a huge smile on his face before getting up and going back to Mummy. I don't know who was more pleased by his progress – him or Mummy and me.**

The walking was a long time coming. Golden Boy had been doing the sofa shuffle for weeks, pulling himself up at one end of the couch and running alongside it to the other end, and usually back again. Then he extended his upright expeditions by using the walls for balance. He would leave the sofa behind and be able to amble all the way into the kitchen and around it. If needed, he would drop to the ground and crawl over to another point of ballast from which he could pull himself up and continue his walking. But if he had a choice, he would move about on two legs.

If I ever offered to help him at this stage in his walking development by holding his hands, I would be stuck with him for ages as he wandered about everywhere. Letting go of him, if I got tired of standing hunched over while clutching my child's hands as he attempted to go up the step in the garden and then back down again *ad infinitum*, would only bring on a strop. He was practicing his technique and was determined to become an expert walker.

That's the amazing thing about seeing my son learn to walk. How he's gone about working it out for himself has told me so much about his personality. For one, he's obsessed with processes and the mastery of walking. He could probably tell long ago how this whole walking business worked; it was just a matter of training his body to gain the strength and balance required to accomplish it. He went about developing the skill in a very methodical manner. He would repeat little feats, like going up and down that step, until he felt he had them mastered. He has a little kiddie car that we keep in the garden and he spent most of yesterday afternoon just getting in and out of it, to prove to himself that he could do it and do it well.

When learning to walk, Golden Boy didn't just wander off into the middle of the lounge and see how far he could get before he fell over on his face. Oh no. He spent time doing the sofa shuffle and the ensuing wall shuffle in order to build the skills, strength, balance, and confidence he felt he required to take the next big step unaided. So, in the days before he decided it was time to fly solo, he would have these little 'Look ma, no hands' moments, where he'd let go of the wall for a few seconds and stand unassisted before falling back against the wall again with a 'Hey, ain't I clever?' smile on his face. Then he'd try to bridge a small distance, like the width of our hallway upstairs. And once he had done that a few times, he knew he was ready for a bigger test.

It was like the moment, I imagine, when the training wheels come off a bike. Golden Boy realised after his first few unassisted steps that he could do this whole walking business no problem, that he didn't need to hold on to me or Mummy, the wall or the sofa, but just walk freely through the lounge while yelling a ka-mikaze-like 'Aaaaaaahhhh,' his arms flapping wildly above his head.

Obviously, he still falls over a lot. When I last changed his nappy I was mortified by the huge bruise on one of his bum cheeks, but walking is just about the only thing he wants to do. If I open the back door to the garden, he's out there like a shot, inspecting the flowerbed and the herb patch and talking to the table and chairs and barbecue, too. Trying to get him back in again is a struggle.

He won't even use support to stand up. This determined little man wants to manage it under his own steam. He won't use a doorframe or a chair to hoist himself upright but instead gets into the downward dog position, with his hands on the floor and his bum way up in the air, then pushes himself upwards and uses all the strength he has in his little legs to raise himself to standing while trying to keep his balance. No wonder he eats loads and sleeps at least twelve hours a day. All that standing up and walking looks like a lot of work.

Crawling, now, is virtually off the menu. As impressed as I am by his walking, I kind of miss it. I wonder if I took enough pictures and video footage of him when he used to do that commando-style dragging of his body across the floor because I know it will never happen again. The crawling era of his life lasted six months tops, but now it's over. Golden Boy doesn't care. He's moved on. The only thing he's concerned with is making the next giant leap forward.

While I would like to take some credit for my son's progress, when it comes to walking I seriously cannot. Everything Golden Boy has learned has been under his own steam and through his own blood, sweat, and determination. He's clever as hell and he knows it, and he uses his smarts to good effect. I can tell from the look on his face every time he goes steaming across the room, he's proud of his accomplishment. He should be. I'm proud too. And it seems that telling him well done just doesn't do him justice.

Music to no one's ears but mine

We were visiting our friends Angela and Alan when Alan decided to get out his guitar. As a professional musician, Alan is quite a gifted player and started riffing away amiably while he warmed up. Their lovely two-year-old son, Elliot, rushed over to Alan and started tapping his head.

'He wants me to play *Head, Shoulders, Knees, and Toes*. It's his favourite song,' said Alan as he started strumming it, to his son's delight. 'We play it at least fifty times a day in our house. Elliot can't seem to get enough of it.'

All of the adults started to sing along and Elliot performed all of the actions that go with the song beautifully, touching his head, shoulders, knees, and toes. He then pointed at his eyes, ears, mouth, and nose, smiling and giggling all the time. Even Golden Boy, who at just thirteen months old was not responding quite as much as his older chum, appeared to enjoy the song as he bopped his body up and down and waved his hands in the air.

Alan continued playing his repertoire of nursery rhymes, from *Twinkle Twinkle Little Star* to *Old MacDonalds Farm*, as we sang the words and the babies babbled and danced in their own inimitable ways. While I know all of these songs by heart from having taken Golden Boy to his weekly Rhyme Time class, I was envious of Alan's ability to just bang out a tune on the guitar with such ease. Many years ago, my old flatmate Peter – now a New Age Dad himself – had a guitar that I would pick up from time to time and eventually I learned to play some basic songs. I was woefully out of practice though, and had never attained the high level of skill and proficiency that my friend Alan possesses. Still, after that sing-along, I wanted to be able to play songs for my son, who just loves music.

If a song he likes plays on the radio and he's near the speakers, he'll lean over, crank up the volume, and start dancing away. After months of attending Rhyme Time, some of the songs we sing there are starting to sink in, too. Of course he's too young to sing them himself, but he clearly recognises them when I sing them to him and he can loosely mimic some of the actions that go with them, such as clapping and pointing at the ceiling and the floor. Wouldn't it be great, I thought, if I learnt to play an instrument so that I could enjoy hours of musical fun with my son, too?

I considered taking up the guitar again, but had some doubts. I was never really that good at it and they are big, expensive items. I doubted if I would ever be good enough to play nursery rhymes on it. When I used to play, I would butcher Neil Young songs. Plus, guitars are just so bulky. It would take up too much space in our lounge and Golden Boy would probably end up breaking it. No, I needed something different, something smaller and easier to play. Then it came to me: I'll get a ukulele.

I had almost bought a ukulele for just ten pounds a few months ago when I saw one in a shop in Bath. It was cheap enough that if I gave up playing it after a few weeks I wouldn't feel guilty for having wasted a lot of money. A ukulele only has four strings, so how difficult could it be to play?

Mummy supported me full-bore with my idea. It would be great to introduce music to Golden Boy from an early age. A ukulele would be fun and they sound so cute, she said. So, I went to the fabulous Duke of Uke on Hanbury Street in East London and told the big, bearded shopkeeper there to kit me out. I came home with a concert ukulele (slightly bigger than the common soprano version and a bit easier for me to hold), a teach-yourself-to-play book, and an electric tuner, because I knew I'd never be able to get the strings in tune using just my ear. At ninety-eight pounds all in, it was a slightly more expensive enterprise than I had first imagined, but having parted with the cash, I was determined to make my investment worthwhile and really learn to play the thing well. Mummy thinks the salesman must have seen the sign 'sucker' on my forehead from the second I walked into the shop.

I tuned the strings and within five minutes had mastered *He's Got the Whole World in His Hand*, which has only two simple chords. Mummy and I sang a couple of verses to Golden Boy, who appeared oblivious to our caterwauling, before Mummy insisted I stopped playing.

'God, I never realised how bloody annoying that thing would sound,' she said, and banned me from strumming another chord for the rest of the day. Now any time she enters the house and hears me happily massacring *Sitting On The Dock Of The Bay* or *By The Light Of The Silvery Moon* (oh, how quickly I've progressed) she shrieks and demands I bring my concert to a halt that instant before she smashes the ukulele over my head.

Even Golden Boy, at fourteen months – an age when one would not think he has yet developed much musical taste – seems disinterested in the device. He used to come up to me when I was playing it and would pull at the strings and flip it over so he could knock on the back of it, but he's quickly tired of that. The other day, when I was playing *Cracklin' Rosie* by Neil Diamond to him while we were out in the garden, he propelled himself from his miniature lawn chair, staggered a few steps, fell to the ground, started crawling, went into the house, closed the door behind him, and smiled at me from inside. He seemed pleased that a thick pane of glass was now preventing his ears from being assaulted by the ukulele's high-pitched noise. My hope of bonding musically with my son over songs on the ukulele has backfired spectacularly.

However, it hasn't stopped me from developing my craft. Mummy rolls her eyes, puts her hands over her ears and shouts, 'No! No! No!' whenever I pick it up, but I quite enjoy the ukulele's romantic, Hawaiian sound. Plus, in the month I've owned one, I have become much better at playing it than I ever was at playing the guitar. Mummy puts it well within reach of Golden Boy whenever I'm not at home in the hope that he'll break it and finally sabotage my playing for good, but he's not that interested in it anymore and merely pushes it out of his way.

I'm happy to say the ukulele is here to stay. Maybe one day Golden Boy, and perhaps even Mummy, will learn to appreciate this fine instrument and all that it has to offer. In the meantime, I'm exiled to the garden shed, the only place in which I'm allowed to practice.

My son the head banger

An accident like that was bound to happen. Still, I was obviously alarmed when I received the text message from Mummy telling me that Golden Boy had a massive egg protruding from his forehead after smashing into a bookshelf at nursery.

It happened just twenty minutes before Mummy was due to pick him up and was, I suppose, entirely predictable. Just one of those eventualities when dealing with a child who is learning to

walk. Golden Boy was careering around the largely safe nursery
room when he lost his footing and – Thwack! – fell headfirst into a
shelf. By the time I got home from work, he was tucked up in bed
and fast asleep so I never got to see the lump sticking out of his
head (it had disappeared by the morning). I'm told the incident
hadn't put him off running; having largely recovered from his fall,
he was racing around our living room less than an hour later.

Toddlers really are daredevils. The pain involved with falling
over every fifteen or so steps and the knowledge that it will happen and happen often doesn't dent their enthusiasm for going
walkabout as much as possible. If adults were that unsteady on
their feet, we'd all travel around on mobility scooters for fear of
permanent injury.

Not so for little ones. Golden Boy tumbles over so often that he
has to fall in a really spectacular way if he is going to cry. Like the
time he went face first into the upstairs balustrade. Even then he
got over it pretty quickly. Sometimes a violent wipeout is greeted
by laughter from him, rather than tears.

Bath-time with Mummy has recently become, from what I understand, nothing short of complete insanity. 'Does he now insist
on standing in the bath the whole time, splashing you with water
and throwing all of his bath toys at you?' Mummy asked, after I
had finished bathing him the other evening. She was disappointed
to hear that he just sat there and played peacefully with his rubber
ducky and that I stayed relatively dry throughout the experience.

I suppose it was not surprising that the following night, after
Golden Boy had chucked all of his toys at Mummy, he then decided to lean over to try to pick them up and ended up doing a front
somersault out of the bath, luckily landing on a thick bath mat
that covers part of the hard tile floor. Mummy said he lay there
for a second, almost as stunned as she was, before he started
shrieking excitedly and kicking his heels against the floor. 'Woo-

Baby Talk, Baby Walk

hoo, what a rush', he appeared to be saying. I imagine he'll be auditioning to appear on MTV's *Jackass* when he's old enough.

All of these apparent head injuries in succession have got me worried. After a child is born, the parents are told to protect their head at all times. The skull hasn't come together and they would be liable to serious injury if anything happened to the head. But now, as a rambunctious fourteen-month-old, Golden Boy seems to be banging his noggin into things non-stop. As well as the nursery bookshelf incident, the balustrade bashing, the bath-time tumbling, and that time he climbed out of his cot, he's had his fair share of brain-busting trauma in the past few months. He even tries to give me the old Glasgow kiss when we're play fighting and he seems to relish banging the back of his head against the kitchen cupboards. No, I don't understand that one either. (Oh, and there was that time he was playing in a box in the kitchen and fell backwards against the chrome bin and then on to the hard laminate flooring, but I haven't bothered telling Mummy about that one yet ... well, until just now.) Just what kind of neurological effect is all of this having? Should I make him put on a padded cap, like the one Chelsea goalkeeper Petr Cech wears, to prevent further damage to however many brain cells he has left?

Head injuries in kids seem to be way too common. According to the British Medical Journal, 500,000 children in the UK attend Accident and Emergency every year with some kind of head trauma, with 50,000 cases going on to be admitted to hospital. That's ten per cent of all admissions. Yet with all these head cases to deal with, medical opinion is split on the way to treat them. Full scan and observation, no scan, just an X-ray, observation only – there is no clear rule on what to do. Some injuries are easy to treat, I would guess. If there's blood spurting from a wound it doesn't take a brain surgeon to figure out what to do.

It seems to be the unseen damage that leaves them flummoxed. A trawl through that great repository of reliable information, the Internet, shows that children's heads are apparently only one-eighth as resistant to bumps and knocks as adult heads. Bashing into a bookshelf could cause eight times more damage to Golden Boy than it would me, if this site is to be believed. Seeing as they had a 1-800 lawyer's hotline advertised on the webpage, I'm not so sure ...

Therefore, I'll do what scientists do and examine the anecdotal evidence. Golden Boy has never, to my knowledge, concussed himself and he seems to be developing normally, so that puts my mind at ease. When my brother, Golden Boy's Uncle Kevin, was little he was always running into things headfirst, such as our family's rosewood coffee table, and he's managed to turn out to be a fairly normal member of society. Maybe we're just a thick-skulled family and these occasional cranial collisions haven't been heavy enough to do any major damage. I hope to God this is the case.

They say you can't wrap children in cotton wool and even if that seems at times to be the only way to protect Golden Boy from nutting a bookshelf, chair, or cupboard door, it is an unfeasible one. I can only hope that now he's brained himself a good few times it'll have knocked some sense into him.

Three really is a crowd in our bed ...

Golden Boy made a rare awakening at midnight yesterday, due to his latest bout of teething pains. He has been stuck on just six front teeth for months now, but as I rubbed Bonjela on to his sore gums at the back of his mouth, I

could feel the lumps beneath them that will soon emerge as molars. From what friends with slightly older children have said, these are the teeth that really cause babies pain.

After the initial soothing that the Bonjela provided, Golden Boy, now out of his cot and in bed with Mummy and me, was wide awake and started demanding that we read him a book. I knew if Mummy and I didn't agree to his request we'd hear his wrath, so I placated his urge for entertainment with a quick blast through *Hairy Maclary* and *There's a Hippopotamus on Our Roof Eating Cake* (his new favourite). With the reading over and both Mummy and I desperate to get back to sleep – hey, I need my eight hours, too – I went to put my son back in his cot, a move that didn't go down too well with Golden Boy.

'Oh, he's not well,' Mummy said. 'Shall we just let him sleep with us tonight?' I knew by her tone that it was a rhetorical question, so I placed Golden Boy between us on the bed, much to the pleasure of my son who wriggled about and made himself comfortable. I knew right away that it was going to be another night of precious little sleep for me.

As a man of some considerable height (I'm 6ft 3in), I'm accustomed to not fitting in most beds. My feet regularly hang off the end of our normal double bed at home. My dream is to one day own a house big enough to have a bedroom large enough to fit a bed whereby I'd need to use semaphore if I wished to communicate with Mummy when she was on the other side of it. I've slept in a bed this big only once, when I was staying at a small, chic hotel in the Lake District. The hotelier said they had to build the room around the bed because they would never have been able to get the frame and the mattress in there afterwards. The bed could have slept twenty. I starfished in the middle of it and didn't come close to touching my bedmate once during the night. It was one of the best sleeps I have ever had.

Now, if Mummy and I had a bed like that at home, I wouldn't mind so much if Golden Boy crawled in with us every once in a while. However, we don't and as he's getting bigger, sharing my limited bed space with him has lost its appeal. Yes, he may enjoy the comfort and security of curling up with us on either side of him to keep him warm, but it comes at a cost to my already shrunken sleep window. There's nothing worse than being woken up at 6am by a slap across the chops from a fourteen-month-old because he wants a nappy change and breakfast. Just ask Mummy (Golden Boy does spare me the abuse sometimes).

I suppose it wasn't so bad when Golden Boy was really little, about six or seven months old. He was tiny and just lay in the middle of the bed and didn't move a muscle. It was kind of cute having him there. We still held a slight fear at first that we'd roll on top of him, but it never happened and Mummy and I became used to sleeping like corpses in order not to move around. Before then I used to be a bit of a thrasher, shifting and squirming in my sleep, never one to just cuddle up to my partner and spoon her all night long. However, after letting Golden Boy kip with us, my subconscious has trained me to stay in one position for hours on end so I don't end up inadvertently harming the baby.

While I've learned not to move about much in bed at night, Golden Boy has done the opposite. He never stays in the same place for more than five minutes. I'll put him down to sleep at the foot of his cot and he'll end up contorted at the other end when I next check on him. He's always in the strangest positions, too. Sometimes I find him on his front with his knees tucked up under him and his bum protruding up in the air. It looks completely uncomfortable. How can anyone sleep like that? Oddly, despite being one long baby (when he was measured at twelve months, he was found to be in the ninety-five percentile for height in his age group) he prefers to sleep crossways in his cot, thus is never able to stretch out fully. I suppose, in some ways, he's still getting used to not being constricted by the confines of the womb while sleeping.

However, all this bizarre nocturnal behaviour proves to be a major problem on the rare occasions he now manages to finagle his way into my bed. I'll put him down in the middle of the bed as per normal and twenty minutes or so later, just when I'm reaching that deep REM sleep we all so desperately need, I'll get a kick in the back of the head. Golden Boy will have managed to jack-knife himself between Mummy and me, always with his head towards Mummy and his feet towards me. To stay out of harm's way as much as possible, I find myself clinging to the precipice of the mattress like a mountaineer to a cliff-face, just one swift boot away from being knocked out of bed, and often with Golden Boy's legs draped over my neck or back. Hardly conducive to a restful night's sleep.

The thing is, we always expect he'll change so the next time he has a mini-crisis in the small hours of the morning, we'll agree to let him slip into bed with us, yet always end up being subjected to the same bed-hogging practices as before. This leaves Mummy and me with three choices: 1) We placate his occasional bed-sharing whims and allow him to ruin our sleeping habits; 2) We play the tough love card and let him scream it out in his cot at 2am every now and again; or 3) We win the Lottery and build a house around the biggest bed known to man.

I think we all know which of these scenarios is most likely to occur.

To the future and beyond ... with yogurt

With Golden Boy now attending nursery three days a week, we've fallen into a happy routine. As I'm normally out of it in the mornings, I can operate on autopilot while I attempt to help Mummy organise our son for the day ahead (although I'm sure she'll be the first to agree that I'm pretty useless) and then I take him on the fifteen-minute walk to the crèche.

After a few weeks of tears and some nasty biting of my shoulder at drop-off, Golden Boy seems to have become accustomed to spending his days there with the other babies, while his rapport with the nursery nurses is excellent. It's heartening to see that they too have grown in their warmth towards my son. He's got to know them and they've got to know him, and they all seem to enjoy each other, which is important. It makes me feel confident in leaving him there all day.

It's also interesting to see what he's learned under their influence. He's only been going for about a month, but the sense of independence he's gained is quite startling. Golden Boy now wants to do so much more by himself and on his own terms. Mummy took him to Canary Wharf at the weekend to do some shopping and let him out of the pushchair while she strolled through the boutiques. Getting him back into the pushchair again was a nightmare, as he kicked and squirmed to escape her grasp. His increased mobility means he can put up a much better fight when things don't go his way.

Autonomy is what he wants and as a parent in a busy urban area, this can lead to some heart-in-throat moments. We took him to a local park for a picnic recently and I almost wanted to put him on a lead. Golden Boy reveled in the wide-open space he could investigate with none of the doors, stair gates, walls, or fences that normally limit him. From the second his little feet hit the ground he was off, seeing how far he could get before we'd come after him. He seemed to only want to go so far before coming back, and I wanted him to feel confident that he could explore by himself, but at the same time I didn't want him to stray too far away; even twenty yards is a long way in an emergency. Fortunately, he managed to stay safe and Mummy and I only had to stop eating a couple of times each before we had to leap into action as Golden Boy toddled off, his interest taken by a dog or a flowerbed.

The dinner table is another place where he now tries to operate on his own terms. When he was little (and it's funny to refer to him that way when he is still so young, but it just goes to show how much he's changed in such a short period of time – two months ago he could neither talk nor walk but look at him now) he would eat anything put in front of him. Not any more. Now he's learned how to use his tongue, spitting out unwanted items of food is one of his favourite things to do. He does it not only because he doesn't fancy what he's eating, but when, say, he decides mid-chew that he's thirsty and wants something to drink. Instead of finishing his mouthful, he'll spit out the food so that he can drink some water. No time like the present ...

Anyway, I was giving him homemade fish pie and some steamed vegetables the other day and, after a few bites, I could tell it wasn't going down well. At first he didn't like the potatoes, then he decided he didn't like the hunks of halibut, then it was the carrots, peas, beans, and sweetcorn he took exception to. I did all the normal things a parent tries to coax their child to eat, from pleading to taking a few bites myself to show him just how yummy that food really is. Golden Boy was having none of it. Finally, he spun round in his highchair and pointed towards one of the kitchen counters. 'Breadstick,' he said, indicating with his finger exactly where a box of them were, before turning back to look at me. I had been given my orders; I knew what to do.

And feeding him? No way. Mummy and I may make the food and put it in front of him but only if he's feeling very lazy will we end up putting it in his mouth. Otherwise, he's in charge, trying his best to master cutlery that he won't relinquish under any circumstance. Golden Boy's new self-feeding method is especially messy when it comes to yogurt, his favourite treat. Just ask him what he wants for dessert and the answer is always immediate: 'Yogurt.'

There are only two ways in which he'll eat it: by feeding it to himself with a spoon, which normally ends up being held upside-down and results in more yogurt being smeared on his face than reaching his mouth, or by dipping his finger into the pot and then licking it. He never used to like licking his food-covered fingers, but now he seems to do it all the time.

'Haven't you seen?' Mummy said, when I remarked on this. 'That's how they let him eat it in nursery.' He's only fourteen months old and already he's succumbing to outside influences.

Golden Boy wants to live on his own terms now more than ever before. As a baby he was more accepting of when and how things were done. Perhaps he was simply unable to articulate otherwise and was physically incapable of struggling too much (although he's always done his best to make nappy changing as difficult for me as possible). However, I'd say it's more than that. With his increased awareness, his personality has finally emerged.

When I first started taking him to Rhyme Time when he was six months old, the coordinator and many of the other parents who attended the sessions would remark on how alert and intense he looked.

'He's like a big sponge. You can tell he's soaking it all in,' Jasnara, the coordinator, would say, after we had sung the nursery rhymes and read a couple of stories. He was like that for the first six months at the weekly sessions we attended. Now I get the sense that he's seen and heard enough, that he can rationalise in his mind what is going on around him, so that he now feels he can better interact with the bustling crowd of children there. He doesn't spend the whole time sitting with me, watching and listening, like he used to. He goes off, checks out the other children and plays. He no longer wants to be an observer; he wants to interact, to be a part of the proceedings, and to make things happen.

Now he's learned to walk and talk, he has the confidence to be his own person more so than ever before. While some children are little bruisers from just six months, getting stuck in to other children and situations, Golden Boy preferred to sit back and watch. Now he's figured out for himself how child society works and has mastered the rudiments of self-propulsion, I can tell he's more confident at expressing himself, whether that's sharing toys with other children, blowing kisses to birds in our back garden, giving one of his coterie of stuffed toys a cuddle, or running naked down the hallway screaming with joy after he's had a bath.

Maybe I'm thick and it's taken me this long to figure him out but I have such a better picture of who my son is than from the day I held this eight-pound creature who had just emerged from his mother's womb. Golden Boy is loving, considerate, willful, impatient, demanding, intelligent, inquisitive, cheeky, sneaky, funny, and energetic, a joker, a showman, a thrillseeker, gentle, dexterous, athletic, interested, tolerant, caring, verbose, alert, incredible, and full of life. He's the most amazing, dynamic person I know and I'm so proud to be his dad.

He's definitely no longer a baby. Yet while he may be this little independent person in the making, he still needs me. It was made clear this evening while I was writing this. I decided to pop back inside from my garden office (basically a B&Q summerhouse that is wired to the mains) to make another cup of tea when I heard Golden Boy crying. I went upstairs to find him inconsolable in Mummy's arms, obviously howling in pain. He had woken half an hour after being put to bed with teething pains, those molars still causing him major discomfort.

Mummy and I sang to him gently to soothe him while we waited for the Calpol to kick in. Here was this young chap who had spent most of his day telling us not to interfere in the running of his life, by refusing to eat much of his dinner and disobeying requests – such as not to throw his shoes into the rubbish bin, not to try to lift up the toilet seat, and not to draw on the walls with crayons – who now wanted nothing more than to have his parents there to comfort him. He may have come so very far in such a short time, but there is a hell of a way for him to go.

Just as I can no longer imagine what my life would be like without him, so much of what has happened in his first fourteen months has been such a surprise for me that I can barely imagine what is going to happen next. Walking and talking, his senses well and truly alive and kicking, Golden Boy has passed some huge milestones. There will be many more to come. I can't wait to see it happen. I look forward to sharing with him all that life has to offer, one tiring, activity-packed day at a time.